Contents

Acknowledgements

Several people have helped make this guide what it is. Useful information has been supplied and sections and drafts of the guide have been reviewed by many professionals and experienced parents involved in adoption. I am grateful for their input, advice and guidance. Thanks to members of Adoption UK, who completed the initial questionnaire which sparked this process, and to the following people for their comments on parts or all of the draft: Hedi Argent, Daphne Batty, Miranda Davies, Lynda Gilbert, Gill Haworth, Marion Hundleby, Mary Lane, Jenifer Lord, Philly Morrall, Shaila Shah, John Simmonds, and Justin Simon.

About the author

Amy Neil Salter is a freelance medical writer by profession and an adoptive mother by choice. This resource guide was born from the databank of services and resources Amy has kept throughout the six years since she and her husband adopted their two children.

This book is dedicated to her parents, who taught her everything.

This edition

This edition has been comprehensively revised and updated by Jenifer Lord, Consultant, BAAF Southern England.

T.

The **Adopter's Handbook**

Information, resources a  *f... parents*

Amy Neil Salter

Revised by

Jenifer Lord

Published by British Association
for Adoption & Fostering (BAAF)
Skyline House
200 Union Street
London SE1 0LX

www.baaf.org.uk

Charity registration 275689

British Library Cataloguing in Publication Data
A catalogue record for this book is available from the
British Library

ISBN 1-903699-62-2

Editorial Project Management by Shaila Shah
Photographs by John Birdsall Photography;
posed by models
Designed by Andrew Haig & Associates
Typeset by Aldgate Press
Printed by Creative Print and Design

BAAF Adoption & Fostering is the leading UK-wide
membership organisation for all those concerned with
adoption, fostering and child care issues

Foreword

Adoption is a mass of contradictions. For every rule, there is an equal and opposite rule. For every practice, there is an exception. For every national statement, there is a local interpretation. What is in the best interests of one child is not in the best interests of another. And so on. How then is the average prospective adopter or adoptive parent meant to survive, let alone understand, what adoption is all about? I'm not sure that I know, but I do know that *The Adopter's Handbook* has a lot of the answers to those sorts of questions and contradictions. As such, it's the best place to be.

Since it was first published in 2002, it has helped many of the thousands of parents who adopt each year. It does this by recognising that adoptive families are special and that the process of adoption is special. Of course, all families – birth or adoptive – are special, but adoptive families can have an added dimension to the challenges of parenting children. It doesn't make the family or the parents or the children involved better people or parents, but it does make them different. And it's important to acknowledge that difference, for it has many practical effects and consequences.

The reason for this is the children that lie at the heart of the system. In general, the children who are adopted today are those who have been taken into the local authority care system, many of them having suffered some level of abuse or neglect within their birth families, and many with a range of special needs that have to be met by their adoptive families.

Because of this, there is a knotty tangle of legislation, regulations and guidance designed to protect the best interests of the children awaiting adoption. And so there should be, but for the prospective adopters who put themselves forward to parent these children, it can be a bewildering, slow and highly intrusive process. On top of that, there is a necessary, but complicated, dialogue that must go on between the social work professionals who work in adoption agencies and the parents who will ultimately care for the children.

Via these hard-working professionals, there is a journey to becoming an adoptive parent during which beliefs and expectations will be challenged. It will be an exhilarating, rewarding and enriching journey, but at times it may also be an infuriating, disheartening and depressing one. *The Adopter's Handbook* is an essential companion for that journey, acting as a clear and authoritative source of information, advice and support.

That a new edition has been published is welcome, not least because of the Adoption and Children Act 2002. Currently due to be fully implemented in September 2005, the Act represents the single most important overhaul of the law of adoption in over 25 years. The Act – which only applies to England and Wales – is part of the government's plans to increase the number of adoptions from care, to encourage more adopters to come forward, to speed up the process of adoption and to provide better support services that reflect the lifelong aspects of adoptive family life.

So, the future holds a lot for adoptive families – a much more pro-adoption and pro-adopter set of laws and policies. But to take advantage of that and to get the best for the adopted children involved, prospective adopters and adoptive parents need to know how the practice of adoption is and will be changing. They need to be armed with information about how the system works, what to expect and what are their rights and duties. *The Adopter's Handbook* will do just that.

Jonathan Pearce, Director, Adoption UK   August 2004

introduction

ADOPTING A CHILD is a "human" process – indeed, a "life" process. It is a process in which adults commit themselves to bringing a child into their home, to love and to nurture, and most importantly, to meet the specific needs of that child. Yet adoption is also a service provided by your local authority or by an adoption agency. As adopters, therefore, you are active participants in that service, and it is in your best interests to know as much as possible about the process of adoption and about the wider issues that may affect you and your family along the way.

The purpose of this guide is to help you to help yourself throughout the adoption process and beyond. So, you may be interested to read this information for any of the following reasons:

Because adoption has changed: Adoption and fostering of children in England, Wales and Scotland has undergone immense change in the last few years and further changes are expected. There has been renewed interest in adoption from the government, the press, and from the parents and professionals involved so closely in the adoption process. There is, consequently, a need for accurate, precise information about adoption *before*, *during* and *after* the "big" event.

Because being informed and aware helps avoid misunderstandings and needless stress: If you know what to expect along the way – for example, the expectations of social workers, the length of time involved, and the potential needs of the child – you will be better able to handle the potential ups and downs of the adoption experience. "Forewarned is forearmed" has never been more true than with adoption – the more you know, the less likely you are to be "surprised" by various events.

Because you will need support and information throughout the adoption process and beyond: If you're just starting on the road to adoption, you'll find that certain aspects of adoption practice may vary from region to region. Use this guide to give you a general understanding of adoption, while asking your social worker to inform you of specific issues. If you have already adopted, you will most likely continue to encounter questions and issues that you had not thought about beforehand. Many adoptive parents often become more aware of specific issues after the adoption – when the initial joys of adopting a child have receded and the parents suddenly are left with "real life" issues to face. Use this guide to point yourself in the right direction to find the information and services that can help you build your own framework of support – as much or as little as you need.

Because you want to help your child: During and after adoption, you may suddenly find you need information from a variety of sources – medical, psychological and educational, for instance. You suddenly need to become "expert" in many areas and need to know how to access the systems and services available to you. There is a wealth of information available. The purpose of this guide is to present it between two covers, so you can seek appropriate information and access to services quickly and easily.

Because you are a "consumer" of adoption services: It is, therefore, in your best interests to have a general awareness of the laws, regulations and practice guidelines that affect social services departments and voluntary agencies. Knowledge of these will enable you to ensure the service you receive is of the highest possible quality. It will also enable you to take action if you believe you are not receiving an adequate service.

Although you are being assessed throughout most of the adoption process, you must also feel free to express your own opinions and feelings – even when they differ from those of your social worker, local authority or adoption agency. This guide provides details of the adoption services you should expect to receive, your rights throughout the adoption process, and where to find help if you have a question or complaint about these services, rights or procedures.

Who is this guide for?

There are many people involved in the adoption process. If the adoption experience has touched your life in any way, then this guide is for you, as well as for:

- **adoptive parents** who adopted years ago, but who continue to confront issues and want to find the best help available for their children;

- **prospective adopters** just beginning the adoption process – use this guide as your "road map" throughout adoption and, later, as backup information as the adoption proceeds;

- **social services professionals** who want to know what adoptive parents and prospective adopters really think and what they really want to know;

- **anyone adopted as a child** and who is seeking information and support;

- **everyone involved with the issues of adoption** or who interacts with adopted children – teachers, mental health professionals, medical professionals, education authorities.

When you have finished using this guide, pass it on to someone else. The more people who are aware of adoption and the issues involved, the easier it will be for our adopted children to live in a community that understands, and is sensitive to, their needs.

Please note that this guide is primarily for readers in England and Wales as the legislative framework, processes and procedures described here pertain to law in England and Wales. However, in many cases, resources throughout the UK are listed – i.e. organisations and support networks in England, Wales, Scotland and some in Northern Ireland. We hope that this will be helpful to our readers.

How to use this guide

This guide is divided into five sections, based on *topics identified by adoptive parents*. Each section is organised according to questions adopters commonly ask. Each section also includes the following standard features:

- **A list of specific topics** covered in the section: this gives you a brief overview of the section so you may determine if it contains the information you're seeking;

- **Terms you may need to know** that are used in adoption, and may be unfamiliar;

- **Helpful resources:** information, organisations and services that can help you to help yourself in meeting your and your child's needs;

- **Taking action:** brief descriptions of current programmes, new initiatives, services and legislation that enable you to be an informed "consumer" of adoption services. This information is not intended to provide a basis for antagonism. It is provided in the spirit of "informed co-operation" – to enable you to work co-operatively with everyone involved in the adoption process.

  In addition, this guide includes three **appendices** for quick, easy access to specialist publishers, books and resources (Appendix 1); the organisations and resources mentioned in each section (Appendix 2); and relevant sections from the National Adoption Standards for England which have been alluded to frequently (Appendix 3). Lastly, an index helps you look up particular topics quickly.

The information in each section is presented in a *quick reference format*, so you can:

- look up information when you need it – there is no need to read the entire guide at once, and

- look for information to meet your specific needs – all children and families differ, so your concerns and needs will also differ. There is no need to read through information that does not apply to you.

  This second edition has been comprehensively revised and updated. The major changes which are described are the Independent Review Mechanism, the statutory right to adoption leave and pay and to paternity leave and pay, and the provisions of the Adoption Support Services (Local Authorities) (England) Regulations 2003 and their accompanying Guidance. The Adoption and Children Act 2002, apart from a few provisions, is not due to be implemented until September 2005. Regulations and Guidance to underpin the Act are being consulted on currently and so cannot be detailed in this edition. However, some references are made to a few of the changes which the Act will introduce.

Give us feedback!

Is there anything you think should be added to this guide? Anything you think should be changed? Any other issues that need to be considered?

Please let us know. The more we hear from the people involved in adoption, the more we can tailor any future editions of this guide to meet your needs.

Thank you!

adoption: your questions answered

1

In this section

- gain an overview of the adoption process and of the points to consider before proceeding with adoption

- discover how the adoption process works and how to work effectively with everyone involved in that process

- find out who can or cannot adopt and what factors are important

- learn about intercountry adoption and about specific issues that may affect this

The children

I N THE UNITED KINGDOM, there are currently nearly 80,000 children in public care. Numbers have risen steadily over the last few years. Being "in care" or being "looked after" means that most of these children are not living with their birth parent/s, but are living in foster care or in a community home run by the local authority. Many of these children will eventually return to their birth family, some of them after a relatively short time "in care". However, some of these children are waiting to be adopted. In recent years, about 6,000 children have been adopted annually of whom about two-thirds, or 4,000 children, were looked after. This compares with 2,700 looked after children adopted in England in 1999/2000.

All sorts of children need adoption. These include infants, toddlers, and adolescents; groups of brothers and sisters who want to stay together, especially if they are older; disabled children; children with learning disabilities; children from different minority ethnic communities – all these children can benefit tremendously from family life. We estimate that there are currently about 5,000 children waiting to be adopted.

Although it is in the child's – and everyone's – best interests to remain with his or her birth family whenever possible, adoption will be recommended when the child's welfare is considered to be at risk if the child remains with the birth family.

How does a child come to need to be adopted?

Figure 1 shows the general process by which children enter local authority care, i.e. are looked after and placed for adoption. A general knowledge of this process can help adoptive parents understand the experiences of their child being taken into care; the time periods involved in each stage of the process; and the attempts by local authorities to rehabilitate the child with the birth family.

When is foster care, rather than adoption, considered best for a child?

Social services departments will consider long-term fostering or a Residence Order for a child if it believes the child will benefit from significant, continued involvement with the birth family, or if the child is older and does not wish to be adopted. In some cases, a child's sense of identity and self-esteem may be strongly connected to the birth family, but his or her additional needs require that he or she be fostered. Long-term foster arrangements may also be considered if the child's birth parents are able and willing to provide some degree of parental responsibility for the child.

Adoption is considered for the child if social services have assessed that the child's needs – physical, emotional, and developmental – cannot be met by the birth parents or by other family members. In order for these needs to be met, the child needs to be placed in a new family that is committed to the child emotionally, socially and legally throughout childhood and beyond.

Figure 1   **Routes by which a child comes into care and potentially to panel with a proposed adoption plan**

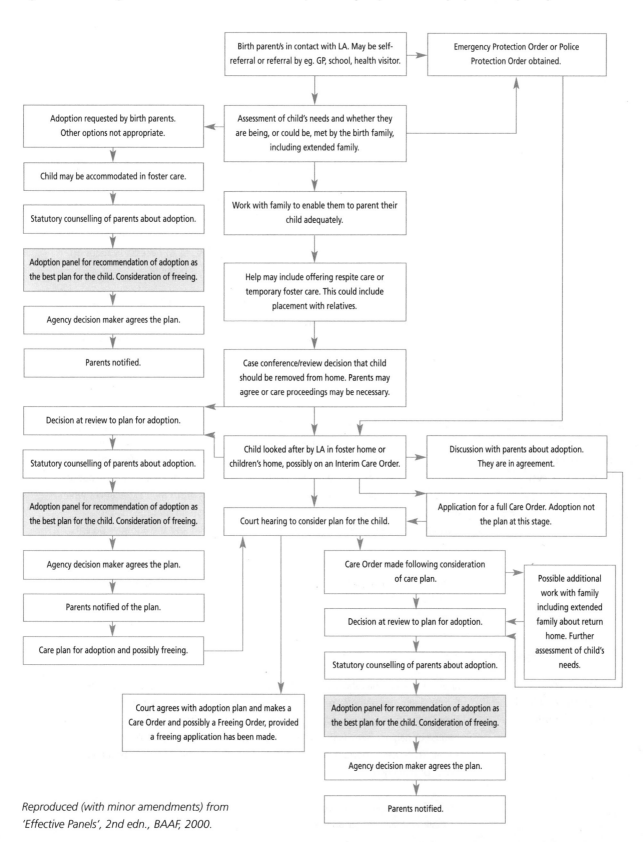

Reproduced (with minor amendments) from
'Effective Panels', 2nd edn., BAAF, 2000.

Is adoption right for you?

'... it will be important for all concerned to be realistic in recognising that long-term and persistent trauma can result in behaviours that are both challenging to live with and resistant to change.' [1]

CLEARLY, THERE ARE MANY CHILDREN who need a loving and secure home, and many more people are needed to be adoptive parents. But this doesn't *necessarily* mean adoption is the right choice for everyone. It is important to consider your decision to adopt in a clear and logical manner – to avoid the temptation to be led to your decision purely by emotion.

The fact that you are reading this guide means you are investigating the option of adopting children. You and your family may have discussed many of the different issues involved already. But if you don't know much about adoption, or don't know anyone who has adopted children, you might want to think about some of the following questions.

Why do I / we want to adopt?

We cannot escape the fact that deciding to have children, through birth or through adoption, fulfils some of our own needs and desires to become parents and to raise a family. After all, this is a natural process in life. Yet most children waiting for adoption have specific emotional and physical needs (see Section 4 for more explanation), and require parents who can commit to being with them through good times and through tough times. The process of adoption, therefore, must necessarily focus on the *child's* needs and on meeting those needs as much as possible.

When you begin the process of adoption, you must also be willing to address your own emotional needs (for example, attachment issues from your own childhood, infertility issues, grief over a lost child, etc.) and must be sure that adoption is not simply a route to overcome your own difficulties.

Is parenting an adopted child different from parenting my own birth child?

Yes. Most children who are placed for adoption have experienced some degree of abuse and/or neglect. And all children needing adoption suffer the trauma of separation from, and loss of, their birth family. These events affect children of *all* ages (even infants) and in many different ways (see Section 4 for more information about these effects). While most children are able to "recover" from their experiences when placed in a loving environment, it is important to understand that the road to recovery can be difficult and frustrating for both the child and the adoptive parents.

It is also important to understand that older children (age 3+), especially, will have begun to develop their own personality and habits by the time they are adopted. As parents, your personality and habits will still influence the child, but less so than if the child had been born to you.

Is it "easier" to parent an older child or a younger child?

Recent research[2] has shown that infant adoptions are generally successful for both the child and the parents. Yet, there is no guarantee that a younger child will have fewer difficulties than an older child. Even babies can suffer the effects of early trauma or neglect (see Section 4). Only you can decide what age child you want to adopt. The most important consideration is to determine how you can best meet the needs of that child.

1 S. Byrne, *Linking and Introductions*, BAAF, 2000.

2 J. Castle *et al*, 'Infant Adoption in England', *Adoption & Fostering*, 24:3, 2000.

Can children who have experienced trauma, abuse and/or neglect ever overcome these experiences?

Yes. Section 4 of this guide describes the many complex emotional, developmental and physical difficulties children can experience as a result of abuse and/or neglect. In some cases, such experiences can affect the physical growth and development of neural connections in the brain and thus affect the child's emotions and behaviour. Studies [3] have shown that, with appropriate treatment (medical, psychiatric and/or psychological), these neural connections can form – the brain can be helped to adapt to compensate for earlier neglect.

When considering adoption, the two key things to remember are:

- providing a loving and secure home will help the child, but may not help the child resolve *all* of his or her problems – you may have to seek additional assistance from a variety of sources; and

- the wounds of abuse and neglect run deep – even if the child was removed from the abusive environment at an early age.

As adoptive parents, therefore, we must look realistically at our own expectations of our child and his or her "recovery". It may take many years (perhaps a lifetime) for the child to overcome the complex effects of early trauma.

Helpful resources

For more information and publications about the effects of early trauma, see Section 4 and Appendix 1 of this guide, as well as:

Attachment, Trauma and Resilience: Therapeutic caring for children by Kate Cairns, BAAF, 2002.
Written by someone who fostered several children over a 25-year period, this book provides an illustration of family life with children who had lived through overwhelming stress and how they were helped to overcome it.

'Early adversity and adoptive solutions' by Ann and Alan Clarke, in *Adoption & Fostering*, 25:1, BAAF, 2001.

First Steps in Parenting the Child Who Hurts: Tiddlers and toddlers by Caroline Archer, Jessica Kingsley, 1999.
This book approaches the attachment and developmental issues that arise when even the youngest child is in your care.

Next Steps in Parenting the Child Who Hurts: Tykes and teens, by Caroline Archer, Jessica Kingsley, 1999.
This book follows on logically from the *First Steps* book and continues into the challenging journey through childhood and into adolescence.

3 B. Perry, *Maltreated Children: Experience, brain development and the next generation*, W.W. Norton, New York, 1995.

How does the adoption process work?

Once you have decided you are interested in adopting a child, the first step is to contact a local authority's adoption team or a voluntary adoption agency to ask for information and procedures. **If you are interested in adopting a specific child you have seen in a publication:** you should contact the organisation that produces the publication for information and then the local authority looking after the child.

When you contact an adoption agency: you will receive written information, or be invited to attend a meeting or an information evening or a social worker will visit you to discuss general adoption issues with you. After this discussion, if you are still interested in adopting, you will be asked to attend **adoption preparation groups** run by the agency. Currently, the structure of these sessions varies, but in general you will attend 4 – 6 sessions, 2 – 3 hours each, over the course of 6 – 8 weeks. After you have attended these sessions, you will be asked to confirm your interest in adopting by completing a formal application form.

The key players

There are five key players in the adoption process:

- the child;

- the local authority adoption team OR the voluntary adoption agency which has assessed you;

- the local authority which is responsible for the child (which may or may not be the same one as above);

- you, the prospective adoptive parent/s; and

- the birth parent.

The courts also play a role in the adoption process, at different points along the way.

Social workers

All social workers in the United Kingdom are required to have a qualification approved by the GSCC or equivalent body. They are required to be registered with these bodies from 1 April 2005. The qualification involves a minimum of two years training, culminating, from 2005, in a degree.

The following organisations are involved in the development and management of the social care industry:

- **General Social Care Council** (GSCC) (see p.17).

- **Commission for Social Care Inspection** (CSCI) (see p.17).

- **Department for Education and Skills** (DfES) (see p.13).

- **Training Organisation for the Personal Social Services** (TOPSS) develops occupational standards and training for employers in all sectors of social care.

- **Social Care Institute for Excellence** (SCIE) develops policies regarding social care, undertakes research in social care, and develops practice guidance, management policies, education and training in social care services.

Each of the "players" have their own "route" to adoption and each has a different perspective on the adoption process. **It is important for prospective adopters to have a general understanding of each of these "routes", in order to minimise miscommunication and misunderstanding with other "players" along the way.**

Figure 2 (p.12) shows a *general* flowchart of the route to adoption of a child, as seen by the social services department of the local authority. Below, we look in detail at the adoption process for prospective adopters.

How can I prepare for adoption?

No one can ever be fully "prepared" for the adoption process and for the eventual arrival of a child in their home. But there are things you can do to make the process a bit easier and to "initially" prepare yourself as much as possible to meet the needs of the child who may become a part of your family:

● Once you apply to be considered to adopt, you will be expected to attend preparation groups run by the agency you have applied to. You will have a chance to explore a range of issues about adoption and children's needs. You can read *Preparing to Adopt*, a training guide published by BAAF in 2002 and watch the video that accompanies it (Appendix 1).

● You can read about the adoption process, so you understand the functions and responsibilities of everyone involved – this helps avoid misunderstandings. *Adopting a Child*, a popular guide published by BAAF and regularly revised (most recently in February 2002), provides a comprehensive account.

● You can gain experience of other people's children – e.g. attend Parentcraft classes at your local clinic or hospital; volunteer to help at your local school, play group or nursery.

● You can meet adoptive parents, through joining Adoption UK.

● You can read about and be aware of the impact of trauma and neglect on children of all ages.

It is impossible to prepare yourself for every aspect of the adoption process, because you can't anticipate everything that may occur. The best preparation is to read about the adoption process and about the children as you go along, so you will know how to access help right away, if you need it.

Voluntary adoption agencies

Voluntary adoption agencies are usually smaller agencies than local authorities. Like local authorities, they are provided with "practice guidance" by the National Adoption Standards for England that, among other recommendations, encourages agencies to '... follow policies and procedures for adoption which are clear, concise and easily understood'.

For more information about these agencies and how to contact them, see:

● *Adopting a Child*, BAAF, 2002 (Appendix 1).

Figure 2   **Process for identifying a family after a decision that adoption is in the child's best interests**

Adoption panel recommendation that adoption is in the best interests of the child.

Agency decision that adoption is in the best interests of the child.

Child's social worker liaises with the Adoption and Fostering Team to start family finding.

Suitable family, approved by the agency, identified.

If none are suitable, contact will be made with other neighbouring adoption agencies, child will be referred to the Adoption Register and child may be featured in *Be My Parent*, *Children Who Wait* or other media.

Child's current foster carers or child's relatives apply to adopt the child.

Possible family responds or their social worker does so on their behalf.

Discussion, visits etc. with family and decision to go ahead. Birth family will be involved as appropriate.

Family is already approved. Contact made with their agency.

Family is not yet approved to offer adoption. The child's agency works with them or asks another agency to do this.

Family approved.

Family will probably meet foster carers, the child if appropriate, and possibly birth parents.

To the panel for matching.

Agency decision maker agrees the match.

Reproduced (with minor amendments) from 'Effective Panels', 2nd edn., BAAF, 2000.

Taking action ...

... to regulate care services

National Minimum Standards for England are in force to specify how adoption and fostering services should be delivered. Adoption services are inspected every three years against these Standards. These Standards complement rather than take the place of the National Adoption Standards (see Appendix 3).

Helpful resources

General information about adoption in the UK

Adoption & Fostering Information Line

An online service that provides links to sources of information about adoption. Also administers LondonKIDS.org.uk, a joint project by 23 London boroughs to recruit more foster carers and adoptive parents.

204 Stockport Road, Altrincham WA15 7UA

Tel: 0800 783 4086

www.adoption.org.uk

www.fostering.org.uk

Adoption UK

A UK-wide support organisation for adoptive parents and prospective adopters with local groups. Also publishes a bimonthly magazine, *Adoption Today*, with news, views, and features, and a supplement, *Children Who Wait*, which features children needing adoption.

Manor Farm, Appletree Road

Chipping Warden, Banbury,

Oxfordshire OX17 1LH

Helpline: 0870 770 0450

Tel: 01295 660 121

www.adoptionuk.org.uk

British Association for Adoption & Fostering (BAAF)

Has offices throughout the UK and provides up-to-date information about all aspects of adoption, including information about adoption agencies and answers to general questions about adoption. Also publishes useful pamphlets and guides including *Adopting a Child*, and a monthly family-finding newspaper called *Be My Parent*. BAAF has information on its website on adoption and on individual adoption agencies.

Skyline House, 200 Union Street, London SE1 0LX

Tel: 020 7593 2000

www.baaf.org.uk

Department for Education and Skills

The Government department responsible for adoption and fostering services and for other services to children and families.

www.dfes.gov.uk/adoption

Tel: 020 7972 2000

Who can adopt?

ALMOST ANYONE CAN APPLY to be an adoptive parent if they can show that they can provide a loving, secure home that will meet the needs of a particular child.

Legally, no one can be denied the opportunity to be considered as an adoptive parent because of ethnic background, marital status, sexuality, or age. You must be over 21, unless you are the birth parent in a step-parent adoption, in which case the minimum age is 18.

Those prohibited from adopting children: People who have a criminal conviction for any offences against children or who are known to have harmed children cannot be considered by adoption agencies.

- Anyone who has been cautioned for such an offence and admitted the offence at that time is also prohibited from adopting children.

- Anyone who lives in a household with a person aged 18 or over who has been convicted of such an offence is also prohibited from adopting children.

- A person who has a criminal record of other offences *may* apply to adopt; however, the social services/social work department will first consider the type of offence, when it was committed, and if the applicant revealed the offence at that time.

It is important to be open and honest if you have a criminal record. Police checks will reveal it anyway and the agency will take very seriously any move to deceive them.

Must we have a "normal" family structure in order to apply to adopt children?

A "normal" family structure is almost impossible to define. You are *not* prohibited from adopting if you live in a family structure that is different from the majority of the population. In fact, recent research[4] has found that some family structures, such as single parents, can better meet the needs of particular children (such as those who have been sexually abused or who may need to interact with only one parent).

Under current legislation only a married couple can make a joint adoption application. An unmarried couple have to decide which of them will make the application as a single person. However, once the Adoption and Children Act 2002 is fully implemented, in September 2005, an unmarried couple – heterosexual, gay or lesbian – will be able to make a joint adoption application.

4 See M. Owen, *Novices, Old Hands and Professionals: Adoption by single people*, BAAF, 1999.

Helpful resources

Lesbian and Gay Fostering and Adoption: Extraordinary, yet ordinary edited by Stephen Hicks and Janet McDermott, Jessica Kingsley Publishers, 1999. Diverse stories from lesbian and gay adopters and foster carers about caring for young children.

Novices, Old Hands and Professionals: Adoption by single people by Morag Owen, BAAF, 1999. Documents and comments on the experiences of single adopters and their children.

'Family building in adoption' by B. Prynn, *Adoption & Fostering*, 25:1, 2001.

'Gay men and lesbians as adoptive parents', by G. Mallon, in *Journal of Gay and Lesbian Social Services*, Volume 11, Number 4, 2000.

We should keep in mind that children have fewer "predetermined" views of a "normal" or "perfect" family. Therefore, their view of themselves as "special" pertains to their adoption – not to the family structure that adopted them.

Here are some answers to common questions prospective adopters ask regarding family structure:

We are long-term foster carers and we want to adopt our foster child. How do we do this? If you have fostered a child for five years or longer, you can apply to the court for an Adoption Order. Otherwise, you can apply much sooner with the agreement of the local authority.

We want to adopt our grandchildren. How can we do this? If the children are in local authority care, you would need to contact your local authority, just like any other prospective adopter, to apply to be approved. Otherwise, you don't have to go through an adoption agency if you are seeking to adopt your grandchildren; you can apply to the court for an Adoption Order.

My husband and I are from different ethnic backgrounds. Will this affect our ability to adopt a child? No. In fact, there are many children of mixed parentage backgrounds, so such families are particularly needed.

My partner and I are not married, but we want to adopt a child. Can we do this? Yes, but current laws state that you cannot apply jointly for adoption. In unmarried couples (lesbian, gay, or heterosexual), one partner only can adopt and the other partner can apply for a Residence Order. This will change when the Adoption and Children Act is implemented in September 2005. From then, an unmarried couple will be able to make a *joint* adoption application.

My partner and I are in a same-sex relationship. Can we adopt a child? Yes. Lesbian or gay couples may adopt just as any other couple (see above) but, as with any other unmarried couple, only one of you will be able to legally adopt the child until the law changes in September 2005 (see above).

I am a single parent. Can I adopt a child? Yes. Recent research has found that some children benefit from placement with a single adult; for example, girls who have been sexually abused, and children who have witnessed severe conflict between parents or those who will benefit from the one-to-one attention and care provided by one adult.

If we had a placement that disrupted, can we apply for adoption again? If you have previously had a child placed with you for adoption and the placement did not work out for you, don't be put off. You may be considered for another placement after a report, written by social services or your adoption agency, is reviewed by the adoption panel.

A detailed look at the process for adopters

Nine steps to assessment

After you have applied to adopt, the main steps of the adoption process for prospective adopters (after attending adoption preparation groups) are:

1   A social worker carries out an assessment (also called "home study").

2   Your Form F1 (see p.17) is given to an adoption panel for their recommendation of your approval as prospective adopters. The agency makes the final decision.

3   If approved, the social workers "match" you with a child.

4   The adoption panel assesses the proposed match and gives or withholds its recommendation to proceed. Social services makes a decision to then approve the recommendation or not.

5   An adoption support plan is agreed with you.

6   You and the child are introduced.

7   The child moves in (i.e. is placed with you).

8   An Adoption Order is made through the court.

9   You can request additional post-adoption support.

Let's look at each of these steps in detail.

1 A social worker carries out an assessment (home study)

The "assessment" or "home study" is a period of several months when the social worker designated to work with you visits you at your home. The purpose of these visits is for the social worker to gain a detailed view of you and other family members in the home, in order to match you as closely as possible with a child needing adoption.

The length of time for the home study to be completed is determined by the agency, according to its own policies and procedures. However, the National Adoption Standards

Helpful resources

Adopting a Child by Jenifer Lord, BAAF, 2002
This popular guide describes what adoption means and how to go about it, including procedures and practices, legal requirements and the costs involved. Includes a list of agencies – local authority and voluntary – throughout the UK (see Appendix 1).

Checklist for Prospective Adopters, available from Adoption UK (see Appendix 2), lists a variety of questions

prospective adopters should consider and should discuss with their social worker at all stages of the adoption process.

How Can I Complain: Making a complaint to the Social Services Department is available from the Children's Legal Centre (see Appendix 2).

Key Issues in Assessment: Points to consider when making decisions about applicants, BAAF, 1998
Primarily for prospective adopters and foster carers who are starting the formal process of assessment.

for England state that the process, from the first information meeting to the placement decision, should not take more than eight months.

The social worker records information on **Form F1**: *Information on Prospective Substitute Parent(s)*. If you already know the child (for example, if you are a relative, step-parent or foster carer already caring for the child), your information will be recorded on **Form F2**: *Information on Prospective Carers for a Specific Known Child*. **Form F3**: *Assessment of Prospective Adopters Adopting a Child from Overseas* is used for a child to be adopted from overseas. All three forms are published by BAAF and most local authority and voluntary agencies use them to record information about prospective adopters. Your GP will be expected to complete **Form AH**: *Medical report on prospective applicants for fostering, adoption or intercountry adoption* (formerly *Form Adult 1*) about you and send it directly to your social worker.

Form F1 (or F2) and your medical report (Form AH) will eventually be given to the adoption panel during the approval process (see Step 2).

Working effectively with your social worker

The goal of home visits is to assess whether you are suitable to adopt and prepare you for it. Although you may feel uneasy and think the questioning and form-filling too intrusive and detailed, it is best to try to approach these visits with a relaxed, informal attitude. Open, honest communication throughout the home visits will help your social worker provide accurate information to the adoption panel. Remember that the social worker needs to ensure not only your parenting skills and capacity,

Taking action ...

... to understand your rights during the assessment process

The National Adoption Standards for England[5] provide the following guidance regarding the assessment process:

● Adoption agencies are encouraged to '... have a thorough and timely assessment process'.

● 'Written eligibility criteria and details of the assessment and approval process will be provided.'

● '(Adoption) panels will receive all necessary information from agencies no later than 6 weeks from the completion of the assessment report.'

See Appendix 3, for more specific information about the assessment process for prospective adopters.

You should be given a copy of your Form F1 (or F2) and you are given 28 days to comment upon its content.

If you have any questions or concerns during your home study, which you feel unable to discuss with your social worker, or if you have particular difficulties with the

assessment process or with your social worker, you can contact your social worker's manager, the Director of the adoption agency, and/or your local Member of Parliament. You may also contact:

Commission for Social Care Inspection (CSCI) From April 2004, this is the body responsible for inspecting and registering adoption and fostering services in England: 33 Greycoat St, London SW1P 2QF Tel: 020 7979 2000 or 0845 015 0120 www.csci.org.uk

General Social Care Council, a new regulatory body for the social care profession in England that sets national standards, training regulations and social worker registration: Goldings House, Hay's Galleria, London SE1. Tel: 020 7397 5100 www.gscc.org.uk

Equivalent bodies for other countries in the United Kingdom include:

● Care Council for Wales

● Northern Ireland Social Care Council (NISCC)

● Scottish Social Services Council (SSSC)

5 Department of Health, *National Adoption Standards for England*, 2001.

and match these against a particular child or children, but also that any prospective adopter meets the legal requirements (see Section 2).

Why do adoptive parents have to be "assessed" for parenthood, when people giving birth do not? Simply because the purpose of adoption is to focus on the needs of a particular child who has had to be separated from his or her birth family – a child who is already born, with his or her own developing personality, habits, and physical and emotional needs. The task of parenting a child not born to you is different and needs to be recognised as such. The social worker's role is to ensure the child's needs are matched as closely as possible to parents who *can meet those needs*.

2 Your Form F is given to an adoption panel

When your home study is completed, your social worker will submit your Form F to the local authority or voluntary agency's adoption panel. The **adoption panel** is an advisory group, established by the adoption agency or by the local authority, which:
i) reviews applications for adoption (both domestic and intercountry),
ii) recommends whether or not it believes the prospective applicant/s can meet the needs of the child and, therefore,
iii) recommends whether or not the applicants should be approved as adoptive parents.

(The panel also makes recommendations regarding other aspects of the adoption process, such as whether a child should be placed for adoption, and if an adoption allowance is applicable; see Section 2.)

What issues will the panel consider when reviewing the application? The panel will review the standard reports (Form F1 or F2 or F3, Medical Form AH) provided by your social worker, as well as information about your statutory eligibility and suitability (including marital status, nationality, domicile, criminal records, and financial considerations). Within this context, panel members will focus on the following specific issues:

● **Your reasons for adopting** – panel members will want to be sure that you understand and can address any relevant emotional issues that have led you to adoption. For example, the panel will ask: Why have the applicants applied to adopt?

Who is on the adoption panel?

The panel must consist of 6–10 people, including:

● the Chair – a person who has experience in adoption work

● two social workers employed by the agency or local authority

● one member of the agency's management committee or local authority's social services committee

● one medical adviser

● three "independent" persons who are not members or employees of the agency or local authority. Where possible these people should include an adoptive parent and an adopted person who is at least 18 years old.

A panel is only quorate when at least six of its members are present, and this must include the Chair or Vice-chair and a social worker in the employment of the adoption agency. Many panels now invite applicants to attend and the Adoption Standards say they should be able to attend if they wish.

The composition, terms of reference and functions of an adoption panel are set out in the Adoption Agencies Regulations 1983 and the Adoption Agencies and Children (Arrangements for Placements and Reviews) (Miscellaneous Amendments) Regulations 1997. Guidance on the regulations is given in two circulars from the Department of Health, LAC (84) 3 and LAC (97) 13. Two additional circulars, LAC (98) 20 and LAC (99) 29 give further guidance on the remit and work of an adoption panel.

Do the applicants understand their motivation to care for this child? Are they able to identify their own needs and expectations regarding adoption? Have they dealt with issues of infertility (if applicable)?

This is not to say that you must have resolved all such issues, but that you are able to identify and understand them, and to deal with resulting feelings.

- **The child and birth family** – do you understand the intense emotional needs of children (of any age) who have experienced trauma, separation or loss? What are your feelings regarding the birth parents and their inability to care for the child? Will you be ready to deal with needs that are not yet identified in the child?

- **Your family structure** – if you are a single parent, do you have a support network you can rely on? Are there other children in the family? The child's position in the family can affect his or her ability to adjust to the family and can be affected by the child's particular emotional needs. Also, research has shown that there is a greater risk that the placement will not thrive if the child is placed in a family that has other children close to him or her in age; an age gap of at least two years is usually advisable.[6]

- **Your relationships** – if you are divorced or have had failed partnerships, panel members will consider whether or not there is a pattern of relationship difficulties that could be repeated in the future and, if so, what plans you would then make for the child.

- **Your age** – while law prohibits discrimination on the basis of age, the panel will want to "maximise" the chances that you will remain fit and healthy well into the child's young adulthood. In order to adopt, you must be at least 21 years old.

Helpful resources

Effective Panels (2nd edn) by Jenifer Lord, Sylvia Barker and Deborah Cullen, BAAF, 2000. Primarily aimed at adoption workers and panel members as well as prospective adopters. Full of useful information about the roles and responsibilities of panel members.

'Inviting applicants, birth parents and young people to attend adoption panel: how it works in practice', by S. Pepys and J. Dix, *Adoption & Fostering*, 24:4, 2000.

Your questions answered ...

What happens if we're not recommended for approval by the panel? It is not the panel that will make the final decision but the agency; the agency is not required to follow the panel's recommendation (see Figure 2).

What happens if we're not approved by the local authority or the agency? If the agency or local authority plans not to approve your application, it must notify you in writing and must give its reasons. You must also be told if the panel's recommendation was different from the agency's planned decision. You then have 28 days to present your views to the agency or to the IRM but *not to both* (see p.20 for details of the IRM). If you do not present your views, the agency can make its decision.

If you make representations to the agency decision maker within 28 days, he or she can refer you back to the panel if it believes your case has merit.

If the case is presented again to the panel, the panel must give the case fresh consideration. Alternatively, the agency may choose (but is not obligated) to present the case to a different adoption panel (some agencies have more than one panel, or may present cases to panels of other agencies). The agency's decision after this second consideration will then be final.

A final decision can also be made, after considering your views, without the case going back to panel.

If you are still unhappy about the process, you may use the agency's representation and complaints procedure.

6 S. Byrne, *Linking and Introductions*, BAAF, 2000, p.18.

- **Your current health** – lifestyle and medical issues will be considered for their impact on you and your family. If you have particular concerns, it is best to talk to your social worker about them.

- **If you have a criminal record** – see *Who Can Adopt?*, p.14.

The panel will also consider issues of culture , "race" and ethnicity (see p.22); contact with the birth family; financial requirements (e.g. adoption allowance, settling in grants [see Section 2]); and requirements for adoption support.

Independent Review Mechanism (IRM)

Dolphin House, 54 Coventry Road
Birmingham B10 0RX
Tel: 0121 766 8086
Email: irm@baaf.org.uk
www.irm-adoption.org.uk
This is an independent review process, conducted by a panel. It is operated by BAAF under contract to the DfES. It applies to cases where an adoption agency is proposing not to approve, or to terminate the approval of, adoptive parents. It applies only to cases in England, and where the panel recommendation was made on or after 30 April 2004.

If you receive notification in writing from your adoption agency that it proposes not to approve you, or to terminate your approval, as an adoptive parent (this is called a "qualifying determination") you can apply for a review EITHER to the agency (see above) OR to the IRM, but not to both.

If you decide to apply to the IRM, you must contact the IRM within 28 days of the written notification from the agency. The IRM will arrange for your case to be heard by an independent IRM panel, which you can attend.

The panel will make a recommendation which will go to your agency. The agency will then make the final decision.

Summary of your rights throughout the approval process

- You must be shown a copy of the social worker's assessment section of the home study (not including the medical information and references).
- You must be given an opportunity to comment on the assessment.
- If the agency decides not to approve your application, it must notify you in writing, and give its reasons.
- You must also be told if the panel's recommendation is different from the local authority's or agency's decision.
- You have 28 days to present your views to the local authority or agency OR to apply to the IRM.
- If you contact the local authority or agency, it then decides whether or not to re-present the case to the panel. It may elect to present the information to a different panel.
- If the same panel considers the case, it must give it *fresh* consideration.
- If you contact the IRM, your case will be considered by an IRM panel, which will make a recommendation.
- The local authority or agency's decision after this second consideration will be final.

3 The social workers "match" you with a child

After you have become "approved" prospective adoptive parents, your social worker will begin the process of matching you with a child or children or you can be proactive by looking in *Be My Parent* or *Children Who Wait*. In some cases, a child may have been identified before you began the adoption process (for example, foster carers adopting a foster child; grandparents or other birth relatives adopting a child; or applicants who apply to adopt a specific child).

Helpful resources

Linking and Introductions: Helping children join adoptive families by Sheila Byrne, BAAF, 2001.
Provides useful practice guidance on the major stages of linking and introductions.

The process by which social workers match you with a child is called "**linking**". As the adoption process focuses on meeting the needs of the child, linking is, therefore, based on matching the needs of the child with the abilities and resources of prospective adopters to meet those needs.

The social worker completes a **matching report**. If you, as prospective adopters, agree that you want to adopt the child (see below), the matching report will be given to the adoption panel. Practice guidance from BAAF recommends that the report '… needs to emphasise the opportunities and the issues for the child in becoming part of this new family, so that the issues can be considered and assessed by the Panel'.[7]

Within the report, the social worker should consider:
- the child's wishes and feelings depending upon his or her age and understanding;
- the child's specific needs;
- the effect the child's early experiences have had on his or her development;
- reasons for the child's separation from the birth family;
- any significant connections the child has with the birth family, foster carers or the wider community, and the adopters' ability to support these relationships;
- how the adopters' family structure and lifestyle can best meet the child's needs;
- what resources the adoptive family might require in order to meet the child's needs (e.g. adoption support services, settling-in allowance, etc.);
- birth parents' wishes (if any);
- other prospective adopters considered for this child and reasons for not pursuing a match with them.

The Adoption Register

In 2001, the Government established the **Adoption Register for England and Wales** in order to provide a wider choice of families more quickly for waiting children. The purpose of the register is to link children with approved adoptive families. The Register is a free service to councils and to voluntary agencies. Councils in England and Wales are required to place all details of children needing adoption and approved adopters on the Register. Voluntary agencies are encouraged, but not required, to use the Register.

Here's how it will work, if you are adopting through your local council:

1 Once you have been approved, your agency should, with your agreement, send your details to the Register. However, your social worker has **three months** to find a suitable match, locally. (This was reduced recently – it used to be nine months.)
2 If a suitable match is not found locally, your referral goes "live" on the Adoption Register.
3 You should be given a self-referral form for the Register when you are approved. You can send this to the Register yourself, if you wish, three months after approval, to request that your details are made "live".
4 The Register searches its database of children and will suggest suitable links.
5 Register staff will send the matching information to the child's social worker. If appropriate, the social worker will contact your social worker to discuss a possible match.
6 If you, the child's social worker and your social worker agree the match is suitable, the social workers will prepare the appropriate paperwork to submit to the child's adoption panel.

The Adoption Register for England and Wales is operated by registered charity Norwood Ravenswood, on behalf of the Department for Education and Skills and the National Assembly for Wales.
Tel: 020 8800 3332
www.adoptionregister.net/AR
admin@adoptionregister.net

7 S. Byrne, *Linking and Introductions*, BAAF, 2000.

Helpful resources

Sources listing children who are waiting to be adopted

The following publications profile children who need families. If these publications feature a child you are interested in parenting, the child's social worker will still have to make sure that you are the right family for that child.

Be My Parent
A monthly newspaper published by BAAF (see Appendix 2) which features colour photographs and a brief description of around 350-400 children every month of all ages and backgrounds from all over the UK. Available by subscription.

Children Who Wait
A listing of children needing new families throughout the UK, updated bi-monthly. Available by becoming a member of Adoption UK (£25 per year). See Appendix 2 for details on contacting Adoption UK.

Adoption agencies also use local or specialist media to feature children needing adoption, e.g. *The Voice*, a weekly aimed at black communities, frequently features black children to attract the interest of black families. Occasionally, for example, during **National Adoption Week** in November, television and national newspapers also alert to the needs of children needing adoption and may feature certain children.

Considering ethnic origin, religion, culture and language when matching a child to a family

In general, it is in a child's best interests to be placed with parents who share as many aspects of their culture, ethnic background, language and religion as possible. Several current studies have shown that these aspects of a child's background play an important role in developing a strong identity and in influencing the child's social adjustment as an adult. Current guidance issued by the Department of Health – LAC (98) 20, *Adoption: Achieving the right balance* – states that 'due consideration' must be given to these areas, but that they must not be a cause of considerable delay in placing a child with a family.

While social workers, therefore, will give 'due consideration' to these aspects when matching a child to a prospective family, they must also consider the adoptive families

---

A question of "competition" ...?

Many prospective adopters are, understandably, irritated when they discover that several families may be considered, simultaneously, for one child. Adopters may feel offended that they have been placed "in competition" with other adopters in such a delicate matter. And, practically speaking, it seems a waste of resources – after all, aren't there hundreds of children waiting to be adopted? The answer is "yes", many children need to be adopted. Historically, however, local authorities have initially attempted to match adopters to children locally, since the authority uses its resources in assessing and approving the adopters in their own area. Many adopters, therefore, might be considered for one child in order to find the family that will best meet that child's needs.

'When considering more than one prospective adopter, social workers will look at the adopters' ethnicity, culture, religion, and language; the child's attachment issues, challenging behaviour, personality, health, disabilities (if any), education, status in family (e.g., eldest/only), and physical characteristics (appearance); the child's wishes and birth parents' wishes; interests/hobbies/talents of child and adopters; contact requirements; and adopters' geographic location'.[8]

---

8 S. Byrne, *Linking and Introductions*, BAAF, 2000, p.27.

Helpful resources

For more information about culture and ethnicity and the needs of black and minority ethnic children, see: *Race and Ethnicity: A consideration of issues for black, minority ethnic and white children in family placement*, by Beverley Prevatt-Goldstein and Marcia Spencer, BAAF, 2000.

which are available and the ability of those families to meet the majority of the child's needs. Many agencies also undertake specific recruitment campaigns in their areas to attract black and minority ethnic families.

When considering placement of a child with a family of different "race",[9] culture or ethnicity, social workers will want to be certain that the prospective adopters recognise that their own experiences may inhibit their complete understanding of, for example, racism the child may encounter in the future. Social workers will also assess the prospective adopters' ability to help the child value, understand and experience various aspects of his or her own "race" and culture of origin, and to promote cultural continuity for that child.

Current practice guidelines for social workers, issued by BAAF, recommend that:

Recruitment, training, support and matching [of prospective adopters] must entail proactive attention to securing placements which can nurture identity and self-esteem; promote continuity of culture, religion and language; buffer and challenge racism as well as meet the other needs of the child.[10]

The child's details are presented to prospective adopters

Your social worker will visit you to discuss the details of a prospective child. If you express an interest in pursuing adoption of the child, the child's social worker and the foster carer/s will also arrange to visit you.

During these visits, it is important to discuss openly all relevant details about the child. Do not hesitate to ask questions because you fear it might seem "impolite" or "intrusive". After all, you are making a decision that will affect the rest of your life

Do siblings have to be placed together?

In many cases, yes, in some, no. Children who are generally placed together include those who have a strong bond with each other and will benefit from staying together as a group.

In other cases, children may need particularly focused attention from the adopter/s, or may have other physical or emotional needs that are best met if the child is placed as an "only child". If a child suffers from extreme difficulties with attachment, placement as an only child may also be less stressful for the adoptive parent.

Sometimes large groups are split into twos and threes to allow families to more easily come forward to parent them. If a child is placed away from his or her siblings, it will be very important to consider arrangements for the children to have some contact with each other, if this meets the child's needs.

For more information about this topic, see:

Together or Apart? Assessing brothers and sisters for permanent placement by Jenifer Lord and Sarah Borthwick, BAAF, 2001.
A practice guide which highlights factors affecting decisions on placements of sibling groups.

We Are Family: Sibling relationships in placement and beyond by Audrey Mullender (ed.), BAAF, 1999.
An anthology that explores sibling placements from diverse perspectives.

Siblings in Late Permanent Placements by Alan Rushton *et al*, BAAF, 2001.
A research study that explores the complexities of sibling placements and evaluates the outcomes in a sample of 133 children.

9 "Race" is placed within inverted commas to stress that categorisation of people into different "races" is a social definition and one which has been used to determine hierarchies which have disadvantaged black people. It is not a biological definition as there is only one race – the human race.

10 B. Prevatt-Goldstein and M. Spencer, *Race and Ethnicity*, BAAF, 2000.

and the child's life. And it is difficult to "learn" everything about the child before you make the decision to adopt.

The child's social worker will provide BAAF's *Form E*, which gives basic details about the child, such as a physical description, his or her background, basic personality traits, and currently known needs. The social worker can provide valuable information and insight into the child's history, current relationships, and behaviours. Social workers are required to provide the most up-to-date and complete information available. Practice guidelines from BAAF recommend the role of the child's social worker, during this visit, is

... not to covertly re-approve [the adopters], but to share as much as possible about the child's profile and to discuss this in the light of the family's strengths and vulnerable areas.[11]

The child's need for services after placement and adoption, for example extra support in school, therapy, etc. should be discussed with you. There should also be discussion with you about the support that you are likely to need and about the services which the agency will provide.

To find out as much as you can about the prospective child:

- Talk to adults who know the child well.
- Discuss the child's assessment (Form E) fully with social workers.
- Ask for a Child Appreciation day.[12]
- Meet significant family members and friends. The agency should have prepared you for the advantages of meeting the birth parent/s even if direct contact may not continue. Many adopters see this as important for the child's future.
- Have access to relevant sections of the child's file.
- Talk to foster carers about ways in which they handle any difficulties.
- Receive and discuss a proposed Adoption Support Plan.
- See also Appendix 3, B.

4 The adoption panel assesses the proposed match and gives or withholds its recommendation to proceed

At this stage, the adoption panel will be familiar with the child's records and with his or her specific needs.

Legally, the adoption panel is required to undertake the considerations and recommendations that are in **the best interests of the child**. Panel members will be aware that they must carefully balance the disadvantages of children remaining in local authority care if applicants are not approved, with the burden of ensuring that the applicants really can meet the needs of the child.

The panel will give or withold its recommendation to the agency, which will make the decision.

11 S. Byrne, *Linking and Introductions*, BAAF, 2000.

12 A Child Appreciation Day is used to introduce adopters to those who have significant personal knowledge of the child (e.g. the nursery nurse, the health visitor); these people often have important recollections to share with adopters.

How long does our "approval" last? Current guidelines recommend that the approval should be reviewed after two years. Your agency should give you clear information about this.

It is important that agency staff have regular contact with approved adopters who are waiting to be matched with a child. Panels have a useful role in reviewing the circumstances of waiting adopters and should receive regular, brief updating reports, perhaps every three months.[13]

5 Adoption support services

Adoption Support Services (Local Authorities) (England) Regulations 2003 and accompanying Guidance came into force on 31 October 2003. These put a duty on local authorities to assess the likely adoption support needs of a child when adoption becomes the plan and to make and agree an adoption support plan with prospective adopters when a potential match is being considered.

A proposed adoption support plan should be discussed with you before the match goes to panel. Once the match has been agreed, you and the child's agency should agree the arrangements for the support which the child and you are likely to need after placement and adoption. This could include, for example, financial support, the provision of therapy for the child, support groups or workshops for you.

6 You and the child are introduced

The match with the proposed child has been approved by the adoption panel and the agency – and by you. Before you meet the child, your social worker should confirm with you information about:

- the child's current relationships (extended family, foster family, neighbours, friends);

- arrangements, if any, for contact with the birth family;

- information about the child's particular needs; and

- any services and support you might need.

You should also take this opportunity to express any concerns or ask questions you may have. You and the agency will then agree a detailed introduction plan.

If the child is a baby, he or she may be placed with you fairly quickly. If the child is older, you will have a series of meetings with him or her before the child is placed. The purpose of these **introductions** is not only to meet the child, but also to help you and the child find out what living together will be like. You can do this by going through daily activities and routines, meeting friends and neighbours, looking at common interests, and focusing on the particular needs of the child.

13 J. Lord, S. Barker and D. Cullen, *Effective Panels* (2nd edn), BAAF, 2000, p.37.

Adoption with contact

Research has shown that in many cases, adopted children can benefit from some form of contact with their birth parent and/or relatives. This can help a child have a sense of their history and heritage.

Contact after adoption may be planned if it is believed to be in the child's best interests. This may occur via "letterbox", in which the adoptive parents agree to provide written information about the child and perhaps a photo, once every year. The letter is sent to social services, from where it is then forwarded to the birth parent. The birth parent can provide information to the child in the same way.

Contact may also occur directly, between the birth parent/s – and/or other members of the birth family – and child, by visits or meetings in public places (local restaurant, park, etc.). It is important that this is properly planned and managed in a way that meets the child's needs. Any uncertainty about this should be discussed with your social worker.

It is important to remember that contact issues should always be decided with the child's interests in mind. Unless there is a court order for contact, adoptive parents are *not* required to agree to contact, but may be advised to do so if social workers believe it will benefit the child. It is also important to remember that, as children grow up,

they may seek to have contact with birth parents and relatives, and may search for them.

For more information, see:

- *Guidelines for a Letterbox for Adopted Children* (1998)

- *Maintaining Links with Birth Families: a leaflet for adoptive parents* (1995)

Both leaflets are available from Adoption UK (see Appendix 2). See Section 4 for more information about resources for adopted people who are seeking contact with birth relatives.

- **'Adoption with contact: a study of adoptive parents and the impact of continuing contact with families of origin'**, by M. Sykes, *Adoption & Fostering*, 24:2, 2000.

- *Contact in Adoption* a new video which features adoptive parents talking about their experiences with contact. Available from Catholic Children's Society, Nottingham (see Appendix 2).

BAAF has also published books on contact, mostly aimed at social workers but which would also be of interest to adopters; for example, *Staying Connected: Managing contact arrangements in adoption*, edited by Hedi Argent, 2002 and *Contact in Adoption and Permanent Foster Care: Research, theory and practice*, edited by Elsbeth Neil and David Howe, 2004.

What happens during the introductions? During the introductions, you will first meet the child at his or her foster home. You will spend a few hours with the child, initially, and gradually spend more time on successive days. You can take this time to observe the child's interactions with the foster carer and to discuss the child's general behaviour and habits (eating, dressing, playing, likes/dislikes, etc.).

After visiting the child in the foster home, the child will spend time at your house during the day and, eventually, may stay overnight and return to the foster home the next day. The length of time the introductory period takes depends entirely upon you and the child – older children may take longer to adjust to you (and you to them). You may also feel pressured by school term dates, holidays, or other activities. But "speeding up" the process to meet these dates may not be in your or the child's best interests.

One of the keys to successful introductions is… the capacity of the adults concerned to work together in the interests of the child… This means acknowledging that adopters bring skills and knowledge to the placement process. Their experience of the child may be different from that of previous carers, as permanence brings with it a far more loaded emotional agenda. Listening to, reviewing with and empowering prospective adoptive parents will generally facilitate positive outcomes.[14]

14 S. Byrne, *Linking and Introductions*, BAAF, 2000, p.10.

You can help the child adjust to the idea of moving in with you. Once you have been matched with the child, you will be asked to create a book for the child that tells about yourself and your family, and what it is like to live at your house. You can include photos of yourself, your home, family, neighbours, pets, and daily or favourite activities. It is helpful, especially for young children, to enable the child to "interact" with the book (by providing crayons or stickers with the book), thus making it his or her own (see *Helpful resources*).

Oh, the stress of it!

Spending time with the child at the foster carer's home can be a stressful experience for prospective adopters. You undoubtedly will be anxious to establish your own relationship with the child and you may find it difficult if the child is fairly attached to the foster carer. In addition, you may not agree with various ways in which the foster carer interacts with the child. **It is important to remember, however, that these first visits are meant for you to observe the child so you can determine how best to meet his or her needs.** Candid discussions with the foster carer(s) can give you valuable insight into the child that will help everyone in the long run.

7 The child moves in (i.e. is placed with you)

In preparation for the child moving to your home, you will have a **final planning meeting** with your social worker, the child's social worker, foster carer/s, teachers – and anyone else significantly involved with the child – to discuss the placement date and to confirm details of the placement agreement. This meeting will help everyone involved to understand each others' roles, responsibilities and expectations during the post-placement period. For example, you will want to know:

- the extent to which both social workers will be involved with the child after placement;

- what contact (if any) the child will have with the birth family;

- if the child will have any continued contact with foster carers; and

- what arrangements need to be made with other services (health, education) and who should arrange them.

When is the best time for a child to move in? There really is no "best" or "worst" time for placement. Generally, you will want to arrange moving in to suit the child. For school-age children, this means thinking about whether the child will need to change schools and when will be the best time to do this. Moving in during school holidays may not be ideal, because there will be less structure and routine in the child's life, which he or she may find unsettling. You and the child will also have constant interaction during holiday periods, which may prove difficult for both of you.

The child generally benefits if your life continues "as normal" after moving in. "Celebrating" the event with large parties or exotic holidays will disrupt the child's normal routine and will make it harder for the child to adjust to the new family and surroundings. After all, returning from holiday or settling down after a party will entail another "change" for a child who has just experienced one of the most stressful changes in his or her young life.

Helpful resources

My Life and Me by Jean Camis, BAAF, 2001.
This is a book that you can use with the child as part of the life story work which may need to be undertaken.

Life Story Work by Tony Ryan and Rodger Walker, BAAF, 1999.
This excellent guide provides insight, creative ideas and exercises you could use to do life story work in different settings.

You will need to arrange:

● an appointment with your GP and/or practice nurse to introduce the child and to discuss any questions you might have about the child's health records;

● visits with schools or playgroups (if the child will have to change to a new one).

Your local authority should inform your GP of the child's placement with you. If the child is three years old or younger, your local health visitor should arrange to visit you. If this does not happen, contact your GP's surgery to make the appointment.

You may also wish to consult the GP with whom your child was registered while he or she was in foster care.

You should receive your child's health record book from your social worker. This lists your child's NHS number, immunisations, a growth record and any other significant health information. If this record book is not available, ask your GP to provide a new one for your child.

Terms you may need to know …

Words commonly used by social workers

Children's Guardian (formerly called a guardian *ad litem*): a person appointed by the court to protect the child's interests during court proceedings. This person might talk with the child and with the prospective adopters to ensure there are no remaining issues that may affect the proposed match with the family.

Curator *ad litem* (in Scotland): has a role similar to that of the Children's Guardian.

For more information, see: *Guarding Children's Interests: The contribution of guardians ad litem to court proceedings* by J. McCausland, The Children's Society (see Appendix 2).

Disruption: a term used to describe adoptions that do not work out. When a placement "disrupts" the child is returned to the care of the agency that originally placed him or her with you. A disruption meeting is planned, followed by counselling for the adoptive family (see also Section 5 of this Handbook).

Later-life letter: A letter written to the child, by a social worker, that explains (in children's terms) why the child was placed for adoption and how the placement occurred. This letter usually is included with the child's life story book (see below).

Life story book: A "book" prepared with the child by a social worker, foster carer and/or adoptive parent, that documents the child's life, from birth, through his or her life in foster care or residential care, to adoption. The information may include a description of the child's birth parent/s and/or birth family, other siblings or half-siblings, where the child was born, foster carers, and how the child became adopted. The purpose of the book is to provide a link for the child (when he or she is old enough to understand it) with his or her past and life history. The book is given to the adoptive parents who use the information sensitively, with the understanding that it belongs to the child. Where no such book exists, you can work on completing one with the child.

When the Adoption and Children Act 2002 is fully implemented in September 2005, there will be more specific regulations about the information adoption agencies are required to provide to adoptive parents.

Reporting Officer: a social worker who is appointed by the court to witness the birth parent's agreement.

Having a child move in will almost be like giving birth. Do I have any legal basis for taking time off work?

Yes. Statutory adoption leave and statutory adoption pay (SAP) and also statutory paternity leave and statutory paternity pay (SPP) are now available.

Statutory adoption pay (SAP) and leave

SAP and adoption leave are available to employees (male or female) adopting a child who is placed with them on or after 6 April 2003. They could be adopting on their own, or with their spouse.

- SAP is paid for a maximum of 26 weeks at the lower of £102.80 or 90% of average weekly earnings.

- Adoption leave is available for 52 weeks but only the first 26 weeks are covered by SAP.

  To qualify for adoption leave the adopter must have completed 26 weeks continuous service with their employer by the end of the week in which they are notified of being matched with a child.

  An adopter who wishes to receive SAP and take adoption leave will need to give their employer documentary evidence to confirm that they are adopting a child through an adoption agency. You will need a Matching Certificate, issued by your adoption agency, once you have been formally matched with a child.

Statutory paternity pay (SPP) and leave

SPP and paternity leave are available to employees (male or female) who are:

- the partner of someone adopting a child on their own; or

- adopting a child with their spouse.

  The child must be placed with the adopter on or after 6 April 2003.

- SPP and paternity leave can be taken for one or two whole weeks.

- SPP is paid at the lower of £102.80 or 90% of average weekly earnings.

  To qualify for paternity leave the employee must have completed 26 weeks continuous service with their employer by the end of the week in which the adopter is notified of having been matched with a child.

  An adopter (or their partner) who wishes to take SPP and paternity leave will need to give their employer evidence of their entitlement and will need information from the adoption agency for this. This is the Matching Certificate, described above.

Married couples adopting together

If a married couple is adopting a child jointly, the couple must choose who takes the SAP and adoption leave and who takes the SPP and paternity leave.

Step-parents and foster carers

SAP and adoption leave and SPP and paternity leave are not normally available to foster carers or step-parents who go on to adopt the child.

Adoption from overseas

Employees who adopt a child from overseas (or whose partner does) may be eligible for SAP and adoption leave and SPP and paternity leave – the entitlements are the same as for those adopting a child in the UK. However, because of the differences in procedure for adoptions from overseas, the eligibility and evidential requirements are different:

- To qualify for either adoption or paternity leave employees must have 26 weeks continuous service with their employer: that is, either 26 weeks ending with the week in which the adopter receives official notification or 26 weeks from the start of their employment.

- The information and evidence which employees must provide for paternity leave/SPP and adoption leave/SAP is the written notification issued by the central authority that the adopter is eligible to adopt and has been assessed or approved as a suitable adoptive parent.

  Both paternity and adoption leave can only start once the child has entered Great Britain.

  It is important to keep your employer informed. You must notify your employer of your intention to take adoption leave or paternity leave within seven days of the date the adoption agency tells you that you have been matched with a child.

  More information is available from:

- The booklet *Adoptive Parents: Rights to leave and pay when a child is placed for adoption in the UK*, available at www.dti.gov.uk/workingparents or DTI publications orderline on 0870 1502 500

- Interactive guidance is available at www.tiger.gov.uk

- ACAS on 08457 4747 47

- Current figures for pay are available on the Department for Work and Pensions website at www.dwp.gsi.gov.uk

---

What if I'm not eligible for this?

If you are ineligible for SAP because of low earnings, short length of service or self-employment, but otherwise satisfy the criteria for Maternity Allowance you could ask the child's local authority to consider making a payment of financial support equivalent to Maternity Allowance.

8 An Adoption Order is made through the court

Helpful resources

Adoption: A guide for court users, available from www.courtservice.gov.uk Tel: 020 7189 2000

The child's "legal" position: The child will not be your child, legally, until an Adoption Order is made by a court (see Section 2). You will have a "settling in" time, during which the social workers will visit you and the child at your home. You can apply for an Adoption Order at any time but cannot get an Order until the child has lived with you for at least three months from the time the child is six weeks old. If the child is a baby, an Adoption Order cannot be granted until the child is at least 19 weeks old.

The Adoption Certificate: Once the adoption is legalised by the courts, the child's adoption certificate is issued. This lists the adoptive family's surname and the date of the Adoption Order and the court where it was made. The child's actual birth certificate remains unchanged and can be accessed when the child is 18 or earlier if the child's birth name and the name of the birth mother are known. There is a short version of the Adoption Certificate which only lists the child's adoptive name and does not mention adoption. Available from the General Register Office for England and Wales or from the General Register Office for Scotland, or the Registrar General in Northern Ireland (See Appendix 2).

Can the birth parents withhold their consent to the adoption when the papers reach the court, even if the child has been placed with you for some time? This is a complex question that depends entirely upon the legal status of the child. If the court has already issued a "freeing order" for the child, then the birth parents cannot withhold their consent to the adoption. If a freeing order has not been issued, then consent can be withheld. For more information about this and about the court process, see Section 2 of this guide.

Can we travel outside of the UK for a holiday with our child, if he or she has been placed with us, but the adoption has not yet been legalised in the courts? Yes. If the Adoption Order has not yet been made, you must inform social services of your intention to travel abroad. Social services will provide a letter giving you permission to take the child abroad. You must carry this letter with you, to avoid any difficulties with immigration officers who may question why you have a different surname from that of your child. If your child does not have a passport, you must have one issued in his or her birth name.

9 Settling in and post-placement support

As your child settles in to life with you and your family, you will continue to receive support from your social worker and from the child's social worker.

Statutory visits: The child's social worker (and possibly your social worker) will visit the child at your home within the first week. After that, they will visit from time to time to see how the child and you are settling in together. The social workers will arrange a statutory review within four weeks of the placement. Another review will follow three months after the first. It is important to view these visits as a useful means of gathering support and information, rather than an intrusive invasion of your privacy. You and the child will gain the most benefit from these visits if you are candid with the social worker and raise the questions or issues that concern you.

What should I do if the child behaves badly during the social worker's visit?
Don't be afraid to treat your child "normally" – as you would if the social worker was not present. Most social workers have had many years' experience with children and will be well aware that the child may be very attention seeking or may behave badly during these visits. It will help your child if your response to him or her is consistent, no matter what the circumstance.

Through a child's eyes ... what do older children feel when being placed with a new family?

It is always helpful to try to put yourself in the child's shoes. How would you have felt, for example, at the age of four, upon moving in with a family of people you had met only a few weeks ago? The child may feel anxious, worried, perhaps somewhat frightened. He or she will need to understand the moving-in process in his or her "own" way. Social workers can help you and the child by giving the child as much information as possible in an "age-appropriate" way, explaining the purpose of the "introductions", and by providing information about you. Many foster carers also prepare the child for this event from the moment he or she arrives in their home.

You can also talk with your social worker about how best to minimise the child's anxiety, for example, by continuing contact with foster family, the child's friends and activities, etc.

Helpful resources

Adopted Children Speaking by Caroline Thomas and Verna Beckford, BAAF, 1999.
This book offers moving and poignant testimonies and valuable insights into what children feel about adoption, including waiting for a family, moving in, and the involvement of the courts.

Adopters on Adoption: Reflections on parenthood and children by David Howe, BAAF, 1996.
An absorbing collection of personal stories that covers assessment and preparation, feelings towards birth family members, parenting issues, and the experience of adopting.

The Dynamics of Adoption: Social and personal perspectives, edited by Amal Treacher and Ilan Katz, Jessica Kingsley Publishers, 2000.
A collection of essays about numerous aspects of adoption. This book is not a practical guide to adoption, rather a collection of thoughts about aspects of adoption.

Intercountry Adoption: Developments, trends and perspectives, edited by Peter Selman, BAAF, 2000.
An anthology that explores several aspects of intercountry adoption from a variety of perspectives including those of "sending" countries, "receiving" countries, adopters, adopted people and researchers.

'Trauma experienced by children adopted from abroad', by R. Hoksbergen and C. van Dijkum, *Adoption & Fostering*, 25:2, 2001.

Also, see Appendix 1 for a list of various books and resources about adoption.

'... there is no single factor that leads to success or to instability in a placement, but the way in which several factors combine and interact.' [15]

Helpful resources

In addition to support from your local authority, the following organisations provide post-adoption support.

● Adoption UK (www.adoptionuk.org.uk)

● Post-adoption centres in different parts of the country.

● Some voluntary adoption agencies.

See Section 5 for contact details.

Support after the adoption: Parenting an adopted child is not always a straightforward matter. There may be problems that crop up many months or years after the child is placed with you (see Section 4). You may have brief questions, from time to time, or you may need specific services and ongoing support to help you with the child.

Settling-in grants: These are available for most children if they are needed. For details about these grants and about other financial supports, see Section 2.

Whatever your needs, the adoption support provided by your local authority, adoption agency, and by other specialist post-adoption organisations can help you address issues you may face along the way. See Section 5 and Appendix 2 for more information about adoption support.

Adoption Support Services

Adoption Support Services (Local Authorities) (England) Regulations 2003 and accompanying Guidance came into force on 31 October 2003. (There are equivalent regulations for Wales.) These put a duty on local authorities to assess the support needs of children and adopters with whom they are making placements and to agree what services will be offered, before the placement goes ahead.

Local authorities must appoint an Adoption Support Services Adviser (ASSA) who has responsibility for ensuring that people are directed towards appropriate services and that these are available. This will include a liaison role with health and education authorities and with local authorities and voluntary adoption agencies.

Terms you may need to know ...

Intermediary services – a service provided by some adoption agencies on behalf of birth relatives. The agency sends a letter to the adoptive parents or adopted adults, informing them of the interest of a birth relative. Birth relatives are not provided with identifying information unless the adopted person agrees. This service will be offered by all adoption agencies once the Adoption and Children Act 2002 is fully implemented in September 2005.

Adoption Contact Register for England and Wales is a database of names and contact information of adopted people over 18 and their birth relatives. Either party can contact the Register. The Register enables both parties to declare an interest before either can act. In Scotland, contact **Birthlink**. (See Appendix 2.)

15 R. Parker, *Adoption Now: Messages from Research*, Department of Health, 1999, p.15.

Intercountry adoptions

Helpful resources

A Procedural Guide to Intercountry Adoption, available from the Overseas Adoption Helpline.

Intercountry Adoption a pamphlet available from BAAF, 2004.

Intercountry Adoption Guide published by the Department of Health, May 2003. Available on the DfES website and from DH publications.

I N RECENT YEARS, more people have been adopting children from abroad. Generally, this trend is due to adopters wishing to adopt babies or toddlers, as there are few babies needing adoption in the UK, or because people have been moved by the plight of children abandoned in orphanages or affected by war or disasters in the countries they were born in.

Pending full implementation of the Adoption and Children Act 2002, in late 2005, the Adoption (Intercountry Aspects) Act 1999 provides for the regulation of intercountry adoption in England, Scotland and Wales. This is supplemented by a new section inserted into the Adoption Act 1976 and by four sets of regulations. The guides listed in the *Helpful resources* box are likely to be particularly useful in this complex area.

● Anyone wishing to adopt from overseas, including parents, guardians and relatives, must be approved as adopters for intercountry adoption by a local authority or by a voluntary adoption agency authorised to do this work.

● It is an offence to bring a child who is not "habitually resident" in the UK to the UK for adoption without complying with these regulations. There is a penalty of 12 months' imprisonment and/or an unlimited fine upon conviction.

How do I apply to adopt from abroad?

You can obtain preliminary information about intercountry adoption from the Overseas Adoption Helpline, BAAF, or the Department for Education and Skills (DfES) Adoption Website (see Appendix 2 for contact details). The *general* process is then:

1   Contact your local social services/social work department. It now has a duty to provide, or to arrange to provide, an intercountry adoption service. It will supply general information and counselling about adoption. It will also discuss with you the children waiting for adoption in the UK. Some applicants may then choose to adopt in the UK; others will continue with intercountry adoption.

2   You must check the specific requirements of the overseas country of your choice. The DfES lists some countries as "designated" and others as "non-designated" for adoption. If you adopt from a "non-designated" country, you will have to "re-adopt" the child after you bring him or her to the UK. Your local authority will be involved in supervising the child's placement and will prepare a report for the UK court that will consider the adoption application. If you adopt from a "designated" country, you will have an adoption hearing in that country and will not have to re-adopt the child once you return to the UK. There are also countries which, like the UK, have ratified the Hague Convention on intercountry adoption. You will not need to re-adopt here if you adopt under the Hague Convention. (These countries are listed in the guides in *Helpful resources*.)

3   Your local authority will arrange for a home study to be done or you can apply to one of the six voluntary adoption agencies which are approved to assess the suitability of intercountry adoption applicants. They all cover specific and limited geographical catchment areas. Applicants usually have to pay for this service. Charges vary among agencies but are currently often £4,000 or more. The home study will cover the same issues as for domestic adoption (see p.16). The social worker will record details of the home study on *Form F3*.

4   An adoption panel will consider your application.

5   The agency decides whether or not to approve your application.

6   If your application is approved, it is sent, along with Form F3 and the medical form (Form AH), adoption panel minutes (if any), and other paperwork to the DfES, or the Scottish Executive or the National Assembly for Wales or Northern Ireland Department of Health, Social Services and Public Safety. These are called the "Central Authority".

7   The Central Authority will decide whether or not to issue a **Certificate of Approval**.

8   If you are approved, the Central Authority will send your papers to the authorities of the country in which you wish to adopt.

9   The agency in the child's country considers your application.

10 If the agency approves your application your name is placed on a waiting list. When a child is identified, information about the child is sent to the Central Authority, which then sends it on to you. You should discuss this information with your agency's social worker, its medical adviser and/or your GP.

11 You travel to the child's country to meet the child. If you are married, both of you must go to meet the child.

12 You must apply for UK immigration entry clearance for the child, and must fulfil the requirements of the child's country of origin (for example, completing paperwork and providing fees, if any).

Will my adopted child automatically become a British citizen?

A child adopted outside the UK does not automatically receive British citizenship, even if both adoptive parents are British. The parents must apply for British citizenship for that child. A child adopted in the UK will become a British citizen if one of the adoptive parents is a British citizen. The exception to this is a child who is adopted by British citizens under Hague Convention procedures. He or she will receive British citizenship from the date of adoption.

Health issues for children adopted from overseas

There may be very little medical information about a child adopted from overseas. It is important to be aware that the child may have an inherited condition that might not become obvious until he or she is older. You must also be aware that the child may have been exposed to infectious diseases, such as HIV, hepatitis B, hepatitis C, or tuberculosis, and that testing for these conditions may not be available in the child's own country. You must also be prepared for the possibility that the child has experienced severe abuse and neglect, and may suffer significant effects from this, even if he or she is very young.

It is important that you are aware of these issues and are willing, and able, to address them once you have adopted the child. A BAAF leaflet *Children Adopted from Abroad: Key health and developmental issues* is likely to be helpful.

Will we be entitled to the same adoption support as families who adopt in the UK?

Yes. Children adopted from another country may have a range of special emotional, developmental, health and educational needs, for which you may need specific services and/or post-adoption support (see Sections 4 and 5). However, you should keep in mind that your child's country of origin will usually want evidence that you can financially support the child, before agreeing a match.

It will be important to address issues concerning your child's identity and self-esteem. You may find it helpful to seek support from groups and organisations associated with the child's birth country.

Helpful resources

Organisations

Association for Families who have Adopted from Abroad (AFAA)
A national self-help organisation that provides phone advice and information about overseas adoption.
30 Bradgate, Cuffley
Hertfordshire EN6 4RL
Tel: 01707 878 793
www.afaa.org.uk

Department for Education and Skills Adoption Website
www.dfes.gov.uk/adoption

Department for Education and Skills Overseas Adoption Helpline
Tel: 020 7972 4014   10am – 12 noon

Intercountry Adoption
Buryfields House, Buryfields
Guildford GU2 4AZ
Tel: 01483 252 525

International Social Service UK
A voluntary organisation that helps families and individuals whose lives are split between different countries.
3rd Floor, Cranmer House
39 Brixton Road
London SW9 6DD
Tel: 020 7735 8941
www.issuk.org.uk

Overseas Adoption Helpline
A confidential information and advice service for intercountry adopters at any stage of adoption or post adoption. Services include an advice line; counselling for families or for young people who were adopted from overseas; training for professionals involved in adoption; and "consultation days" for prospective intercountry adopters.
64 – 66 High Street
Barnet
Hertfordshire EN5 5SJ
Tel: 0870 516 8742
email: info@oah.org.uk
www.oah.org.uk

Overseas Adoption Support and Information Service (OASIS)
A self-help group that provides information and advice for intercountry adopters, as well as post-adoption support. Produces leaflets and a newsletter, operates an advice line and conducts seminars.
Tel: 0870 241 7069
www.adoptionoverseas.org.uk

In addition to the organisations listed here, there are organisations for families who have adopted from particular countries (for example, Children Adopted from China (CAC) and the Adopted Romanian Children's Society (ARC)). Contact the Overseas Adoption Helpline for more information about these groups.

legal and financial matters

2

In this section

•

gain a general understanding
of the current laws and
regulations concerning
adoption and how they may
affect you

•

learn about your legal rights
throughout the adoption
process and afterwards, and
about the rights of the child
and the birth parents

•

find out about the various
costs involved with adoption
and the financial assistance
that may be available to some
applicants

Introduction

The Adoption and Children Act 2002 will not be implemented, in the main, until September 2005. It will change significant parts of the adoption process, particularly in relation to planning for children. It will be underpinned by new regulations, which are currently in draft form and being consulted on. They should be finalised and issued by early 2005. The Act is available, and the regulations will be, from The Stationery Office.
Tel: 0845 702 3474
email: book.orders@tso.co.uk

ADOPTING A CHILD is a legal process governed by rules and regulations designed to protect everyone involved in the process – most importantly the child, but also the adoptive parents and the birth parents. These laws are designed not only to protect you (and others), but also to help you safeguard your interests. Understanding your legal entitlements and obligations throughout the adoption process, therefore, can help you to be prepared and informed consumers every step of the way.

Before we look at your legal entitlements and obligations throughout the adoption process, it helps to understand the laws that underpin these rights. The main laws in England and Wales are as follows:

The Adoption Act 1976 consolidated former Adoption Acts and the adoption provision of the Children Act 1975. It is the only statute governing adoption, although some of its provisions have been amended by the Children Act 1989.

The Children Act 1989 made the welfare of the child paramount and includes basic principles, such as the definition of parental responsibility and the principles to be followed by the courts in making decisions in children's cases; orders providing for the care and maintenance of children; and the responsibilities of local authorities for children. It also amended many other Acts. It is the major statute dealing with child care law, and came into force on 14 October 1991.

The Human Rights Act 1998 gives effect in the UK to rights and freedoms guaranteed under the European Convention on Human Rights.

Helpful resources

- **Child Care Law: A summary of the law in England and Wales** by Deborah Cullen and Mary Lane, BAAF, 2003 (4th edition). A popular quick reference guide to the law in England and Wales relating to the care of children.

- **Child Care Law: Scotland** by Alexandra Plumtree, BAAF, 1997.

- **Adoption Now: Law, regulations, guidance and standards** by Fergus Smith and Roy Stewart with Deborah Cullen, BAAF, 2003. A handy guide to all adoption legislation.

- **Court Service website**
  The application form for an Adoption Order can be printed from www.courtservice.gov.uk.

- **Department for Education and Skills Adoption Website**
  www.dfes.gov.uk/adoption

For written copies of legislation and explanatory notes about current legislation in the United Kingdom, contact:

- **Her Majesty's Stationery Office (HMSO)**
  St Clement's House, 2 – 16 Colegate
  Norwich NR3 1BQ
  or access the information on www.hmso.gov.uk

- **The Stationery Office**
  PO Box 29, Norwich NR3 1GN
  Tel: 0845 702 3474 – to purchase copies of legislation
  Tel: 0870 600 5522 – general enquiries.

Taking action ...

... Current initiatives in developing National Adoption Standards

National Adoption Standards for England were published by the Department of Health in August 2001. These standards are designed to improve the quality of adoption practice by informing *everyone* involved in adoption (including children, adopters, birth parents, local authority and voluntary adoption agencies) of what they can expect regarding issues such as timescales for placing children, matching children and families, the decision-making process, and access to services (including adoption support). The Standards have the force of formal Guidance from 1 April 2003.

The Adoption (Intercountry Aspects) Act 1999, finally implemented in June 2003, enabled the UK to ratify the 1993 Hague Convention on the Protection of Children and Co-operation in Respect of Intercountry Adoption. The Convention ensures that the welfare of children is paramount in intercountry adoption.

The Protection of Children Act 1999 provides a cross-sector system for identifying people who are considered unsuitable to work with children and establishes the Criminal Records Bureau (CRB).

The Care Standards Act 2000 governs the inspection and registration of fostering and adoption services. From April 2004 these functions are carried out by the Commission for Social Care Inspection (CSCI).

There also are many Regulations that affect adoption, for example, Adoption Agencies Regulations 1983 (SI 1983/64), which govern the way in which adoption agencies carry out their functions (including the function of adoption panels); and those that prohibit agencies from approving adopters or foster carers who have been convicted or have been cautioned for "specified offences" such as abuse of children. The Adoption Support Services (Local Authorities) (England) Regulations 2003 detail new adoption support arrangements.

Terms you may need to know

Adoption Order A court order that transfers sole parental responsibility to the adoptive parent/s. An Adoption Order usually cannot be made unless the child and adopters attend the Adoption Order hearing at court (unless there are special circumstances preventing the child or one of the adopters from attending). The court can attach conditions or other orders to the Adoption Order (for example, contact with the birth family or significant persons, or requirements for the child's religious upbringing) although this is rare.

If the court refuses the Adoption Order, the adoption agency (if it is an agency placement) is entitled to issue a notice requiring the child to be returned to the agency within 7 days.

Care Order A court order giving a local authority parental responsibility for a child which is shared with the child's birth parents, but enables the local authority to make the major decisions about a child's life, such as with whom and where the child should live, and consent to routine medical treatment.

Contact Order There are two types of Contact Orders:

- *Section 34 Contact Order – Children Act 1989* is a court order that determines if a child who is subject to a Care Order will or will not have contact with his or her birth family, and in what circumstances.
- *Section 8 Contact Order – Children Act 1989* is a court order that determines if a child who is living with one birth parent or relative and is separated from the other birth parent or relative, will or will not have contact, and in what circumstances. Birth parents whose child has been freed for adoption or who is adopted may also apply for this type of Contact Order.

Emergency Protection Order A court order allowing social services, in an emergency, either to keep a child in a safe place (such as a hospital or foster home) or to remove a child (e.g. from home) if it is considered the child is suffering, or is at risk of suffering, significant harm. Social services must then apply to the court for a Care Order within the next 7 days, if it is believed the child should remain in care to safeguard his or her welfare.

For both an Emergency Protection Order and a Care Order to be granted by a court, social services must satisfy the court that the child is suffering, or is at risk of suffering, significant harm, attributable to an unsatisfactory standard of parental care.

Children's Guardian An officer (formerly called a guardian *ad litem*) appointed by a court when:
i) an application is made by a local authority for a Care Order or a Supervision Order for a child; or
ii) when an application is made for a Freeing for Adoption Order or an Adoption Order which is likely not to be agreed by the birth parents.
A Children's Guardian may also be appointed in adoption proceedings in other circumstances, for example, if a child has no living birth parents or has significant disabilities. The Children's Guardian is an experienced qualified social worker independent of the local authority.

The Children's Guardian conducts an independent investigation to establish whether or not the order applied for is in the interests of the child. He or she meets with the child, the adopters, the social worker/s and the birth parents. The Children's Guardian may also make other relevant investigations, if necessary. He or she then presents the findings to the court, which will then either grant or refuse the adoption.

Freeing Order A court order that ends parents' parental responsibility and transfers parental responsibility to the local authority. The purpose of this is to allow any issue regarding parental consent to be resolved before the child is placed with prospective adopters or before adopters apply for an Adoption Order. A Freeing Order also ends the legal duty of a local authority to provide contact with the birth family. Birth parents can apply to court to have the order revoked if the child has not been placed for adoption a year after the freeing order was made.

Parental Responsibility includes all the rights, duties, powers and responsibilities which by law a parent has in relation to a child. When a child is born to married parents, both have parental responsibility; if the parents are unmarried, the mother alone has parental responsibility but the father may acquire it by formal agreement with the mother or by a court order or, from December 2003, if they jointly register the birth with the mother. Others acquire parental responsibility by adoption – in which case the adoptive parents acquire all the responsibility formerly held by the parents; by being appointed guardians – in which case they hold the full parental responsibility that a parent would have under a residence order; and in the case of a local authority:
- by the making of a Care Order, in which case the parent's or guardian's parental responsibility is not lost;
- or an Emergency Protection Order, which gives the applicant parental responsibility subject to considerable restrictions;
- or a Freeing Order for adoption in which case parental responsibility is transferred to the adoption agency.

Reporting Officer An officer appointed by a court when an application is made for a Freeing for Adoption or Adoption Order with which the birth parents agree. The Reporting Officer ensures the parent/s fully understand the legal effect of the order and have given their agreement willingly and unconditionally; the Reporting Officer then witnesses the birth parent/s' signed agreement and prepares a report for the court. After speaking with the Reporting Officer, or at any point during the proceedings, if one or both of the birth parents decides not to agree to the adoption/freeing, then the court appoints a Children's Guardian.

Residence Order A court order that determines with whom a child will live, if separated parents cannot agree this. Residence Orders are sometimes granted to other relatives such as grandparents. The making of a Residence Order discharges a Care Order. The holder of a Residence Order shares parental responsibility for the child, along with the child's parents.

Supervision Order A court order which places the child under the supervision of the local authority. The supervisor's duty is to "advise, assist and befriend" and the court may attach certain requirements to the order. A Supervision Order does not give the local authority parental responsibility.

Summary of the legal entitlements and legal requirements of people involved in the adoption process

Everyone involved in the adoption process, including birth parents and adoptive parents, has legal entitlements throughout the process, but must also meet the legal requirements of legislation and regulations. These entitlements and requirements are listed in the table below.

Persons involved	Legal requirements	Legal entitlements
The child	• A child cannot be adopted once he or she has reached 18 years of age, or is married. • Before a child can be placed with adoptive parents by an adoption agency, the child's circumstances must be considered, in compliance with regulations, by the agency. The agency must take into account the recommendations of the adoption panel and a decision must be reached about: i) whether adoption is in the child's best interests and ii) whether a Freeing for Adoption Order should be applied for. • Children placed for adoption within the UK must be placed by an approved adoption agency, unless the placement is with a close relative. • The proposed match between the child and prospective adopters must also be approved by the agency, which will take into account the recommendations of the adoption panel. • The child's need for support services after placement and adoption must be assessed and a plan made.	• The welfare of the child must be the first consideration of everyone involved in making any decisions about adoption. • The child's wishes and feelings about adoption decisions must be given full consideration, taking into account the child's age and ability to understand the issues. In Scotland, children must give written consent to adoption at the age of 12 years. • All adoptions are registered in the **Adopted Children Register**. At age 18, the adopted person may apply to the Registrar General to obtain a copy of his or her original birth certificate. This is available to adopted persons in Scotland at the age of 16. If adopted before 12 November 1975, the adopted person must attend an interview with a counsellor before the birth certificate is made available. • At the age of 18, the adopted person may apply to the Registrar General to be given the name(s) of registered birth relatives listed in the **Adoption Contact Register** as wishing to have contact with the adopted person. It must be the adopted person who decides whether or not to contact the relative.

Persons involved	Legal requirements	Legal entitlements
Prospective adopters/ adoptive parents	• Must be at least 21 years of age and domiciled in the UK, in order to adopt a child.	• Prospective adopters are entitled to a fair and prompt service from adoption agencies, in accordance with the **National Adoption Standards for England**.
	• If the birth parent of a child is adopting with his or her spouse (known as step-parent adoption), the birth parent need only be 18 years old.	• Are entitled to comment and make representations about their assessment by the adoption agency.
	• There is no legal upper age limit although adoption agencies can and do apply maximum age limits – these are often flexible.	• Are entitled to be assessed for support and assistance (including financial assistance, in some cases) after placement and adoption.
	• Must not have a conviction or caution for "specified offences" as described in Section 1 (*Who Can Adopt?*) of this guide.	• If the child has been made the subject of a Care Order or Freeing Order for Adoption, the birth parent/s of the child cannot remove the child from the adopters without the permission of the local authority holding the Order.
	• Single people can adopt, but two people living together must be legally married to adopt jointly. This will change when the Adoption and Children Act 2002 is fully implemented in September 2005	• If the child is placed with prospective adopters and they have filed their application for an Adoption Order in court, neither the birth parent/s nor the adoption agency can remove the child from the adopters' home without the adopters' permission or the permission of the court, whatever the child's legal status.
	• Must be assessed and approved by a UK adoption agency, after taking into account the recommendations of the adoption panel, as well as medical information and other checks regarding suitability (see Section 1 for detailed information).	• Prospective adopters can file their application for an Adoption Order as soon as the child is placed with them by an adoption agency, although the order cannot be granted by a court until the child is 19 weeks old and has lived with the adopters for the 13 weeks preceding the granting of the Adoption Order.
	• Must allow sufficient opportunities for agency social workers and others to visit their home after the child has been placed, to ensure the child's welfare. Those adopting through a local authority agency must also allow the agency to undertake statutory reviews of the placement.	• Once the court has granted the Adoption Order, the adoptive parents have sole parental responsibility for the child. Any previous court orders regarding the child are discharged.
	• Those adopting children from overseas must comply with regulations for their approval and for notification of their local authority (see Section 1 for details).	• If prospective adopters do not wish to continue to care for the child placed with them, they can ask for the child to be returned to the agency, which must receive the child.
	• Prospective adopters do not have parental responsibility for the child placed with them until an Adoption Order is granted (unless one of the adopters is a birth parent of the child and has parental responsibility). This will change when the Adoption and Children Act 2002 is fully implemented in September 2005.	

Persons involved	Legal requirements	Legal entitlements
Birth parents	Birth fathers who are not married to the birth mother can acquire parental responsibility by agreement or by court order or, from December 2003, by jointly registering the birth with the mother. Only birth parents who have parental responsibility for a child can give or withhold legal agreement to the making of an Adoption Order or Freeing Order. If agreement is not given, the court can be asked to dispense with it, if certain legal grounds are proved. Agreement to the making of an Adoption Order or Freeing Order must be given freely, unconditionally and with full understanding. Evidence of that agreement must be available to the court. Agreement cannot be given by a birth mother until the child is six weeks old. The birth mother's age is not a factor. A birth mother cannot be compelled by law to disclose the identity of the birth father or her own family members.	Birth mothers acquire parental responsibility for their child automatically at the birth, as does a birth father married to the birth mother. If a birth mother voluntarily relinquishes her child to an agency for adoption, she and a birth father with parental responsibility retain parental responsibility for the child. This entitles her/them to remove the child from the agency's care or from the adoptive placement, unless the adopters have applied to the court for an Adoption Order or unless the agency is granted an Emergency Protection Order or a Care Order by a court. All birth parents are entitled to contact with their child after the child is placed for adoption, until the Adoption Order has been granted. Contact may be refused only if the agency has been granted: i) Order for Permission to Refuse Contact (section 34[4] Children Act 1989); or ii) Freeing for Adoption Order (section 18 Adoption Act 1976). All birth parents must be notified of any decisions made by the agency about their child. This includes: i) that adoption is in the child's best interests; ii) the placement of their child for adoption; and iii) that an Adoption Order has been granted. Unless a child has been freed for adoption, birth parents with parental responsibility are parties to the adoption proceedings, and the court can hear their views. Increasingly, birth fathers without parental responsibility will be made parties to adoption and freeing proceedings.

Persons involved	Legal requirements	Legal entitlements
Local authority/ adoption agency (this information *does not* apply to step-parent or overseas adopters)	• The agency must ascertain the wishes and feelings of the birth parents about the adoption and about the child's religious and cultural upbringing. The agency must place the child, as far as is practicable, according to these views. • If the whereabouts or identity of the birth father is unknown, the agency must try, so far as is practicable, to find him and seek his views about the proposed adoption (unless this is contrary to the welfare of the child). • If the child is the subject of an application for a Freeing for Adoption Order, the agency must also determine, so far as is practicable, if the birth father intends to apply for a Residence Order or for a Parental Responsibility Order. • The agency must prepare, and agree with the adopters, an Adoption Support Plan. • The agency must inform the local authority in whose area the child is placed, and the health authority, local education authority and the adopter's GP when a child is placed. • The agency must visit the child in the adoptive home within one week of placement, and regularly thereafter. It must review the placement within four weeks of placement, again at three months after placement, and thereafter at six-monthly intervals until an Adoption Order is granted. • When the application for an Adoption Order/Freeing for Adoption Order is filed at court, the agency must prepare a court report (known as a Schedule 2 report) concerning the background of the child and birth family, and the adopters[s], the child's welfare in placement for adoption, the reasons for the agency's decision making, and the agency's opinion as to whether the order applied for is in the child's best interests.	• The agency does not have parental responsibility for a child who is voluntarily relinquished for adoption, unless subsequently acquired by a court order. • If the agency holds a Care Order for the child, it shares parental responsibility with the children's birth parents, but has the power to make major decisions about the child (such as where the child lives and with whom), even if this is against the birth parents' wishes. • If the agency holds a Freeing for Adoption Order for the child, then it has sole parental responsibility for that child, and is entitled to refuse contact until and unless a section 8 Contact Order (Children Act 1989) is granted by a court. • The local authority holding a Care Order or Freeing for Adoption Order is a party to the application for an Adoption Order and can have its views heard by the court on that application.

The role of the courts in the adoption process

THE ROLE OF THE COURTS throughout the process of adoption is to ensure that the welfare of the child is the court's first consideration and that the legal rights of all parties involved in the process (especially the child's rights) are protected.

Three different courts can undertake adoption proceedings:

- Magistrates Court (known as the Family Proceedings Court)

- County Court Adoption Centres

- High Court

What is the general process for applying for an Adoption Order?

To apply for an Adoption Order, you must file an application with the court. If a court has previously made orders involving the child (such as a Care Order or Freeing Order), then the application for an Adoption Order should be filed in that same court. The application can subsequently be transferred to another court, e.g. closer to your home area or a County Court Adoption Centre.

You may not require legal advice or representation to file the application if:

- the birth parents agree to making an Adoption Order for the child

OR

- the child is freed for adoption

Usually, staff from your adoption agency will assist you with making the application and providing some of the accompanying documents.

You will almost certainly require legal advice and assistance if there is any chance that the birth parents will not agree to the application, or will contest it. It is vital to consult a solicitor who has experience in adoption law.

If your adoption agency or local authority has parental responsibility for the child (through a Care Order or Freeing Order), then it may meet your legal costs. If you are on a very low income you may be eligible for public funding to pay legal costs; your solicitor will advise about this.

If you do not wish your identity to be disclosed to the birth family, you can ask the court for a serial number which replaces your name and address on the application and court documents.

The following documents must be filed at the court, along with your application. The application must be filed in triplicate on a standard court form. If the application is not likely to be agreed by the birth parents you must also file a "statement of facts" in triplicate (see below).

Helpful resources

Adoption: A guide for court users
www.courtservice.gov.uk
Tel: 020 7189 2000
The Court Service
Clive House
Petty France
London SW1H 9HD

- your marriage certificate (unless you are a single adopter)*

- a decree absolute, if you have been divorced*

- the child's birth certificate*

- a copy of any previous court orders (such as a Care Order or Freeing Order) that the child is subject to

- if the child has not been freed for adoption, any documents available to you (usually in step-parent and intercountry adoptions) that show the birth parent/s have agreed to the adoption

- your adoption agency (or local authority, for step-parent or intercountry adoptions) will file a Schedule 2 report at the court when the court notifies the agency of your application.

There is a court fee for the application. Currently, the fee is £30 per child in the Magistrates Court and £120 per child in the County Court and High Court. If the child has been placed for adoption by an adoption agency, which is supporting the application, the agency is expected to pay the court fee.

If the birth parents agree to the application for an Adoption Order, the court will appoint a Reporting Officer. This person interviews the birth parents, ensures that they give their agreement willingly, unconditionally and with full understanding, and if so, witnesses their written agreement.

These must not be photocopies

What happens if the birth parent/s contest the adoption?

If the birth parents contest or do not agree to the application:

- You are required to ask the court (via your solicitor if you have one) to dispense with the birth parents' agreement. This is done by filing with your application a "statement of facts" (in triplicate) setting out the child's past and current circumstances and the reasons why you believe the legal grounds for dispensing with parental agreement are met. The statement of facts should be prepared by your solicitor or by the Legal Department of the local authority if the child is in care. Legal

Taking action ...

... to speed up the court process in adoption

The DfES has been working with the Department for Constitutional Affairs (which is responsible for courts in England and Wales) to speed up the legal process of adoption. This is being achieved with several initiatives, including: increasing the number of judges dealing with family work; making better use of judges and magistrates with expertise in adoption; finding new ways to manage adoption cases and thus reduce delay; and improving communication between everyone involved in the court adoption process.

Adoption Centres have been established in England and Wales to centralise all adoption work from county courts. The centres will have specialist judiciary and staff who are experienced in adoption proceedings. These centres are part of the government guidance, *Adoption Proceedings – a new approach*, that aims to reduce delay and to improve the services provided by the courts. If you have made an application to a County Court which is not an Adoption Centre, the application will be transferred by the court.

grounds for dispensing with consent must be proved to the court. The ground (see section 16 Adoption Act 1976) most commonly used is that the birth parents are 'withholding consent unreasonably'.

● The court will appoint a **Children's Guardian** to examine all aspects of the Adoption Order application and to prepare a report advising the court as to whether the Adoption Order is in the best interests of the child. The Guardian will interview you, the birth parent/s, the social workers and, probably, the child. The Guardian will also undertake any other investigation considered necessary or ordered by the court.

When must adopters attend court proceedings and why?

There are two types of court hearings: "directions hearings" and the final hearing for the Adoption Order application. You may not be required to attend directions hearings, but it is usually best to do so, subject to your solicitor's advice. You are required to attend the final hearing.

Directions hearings There may be several brief court hearings before the final hearing at which the application for the Adoption Order is decided. These directions hearings enable the court to advise you and/or your solicitor (and other parties) about procedural and evidential matters which need to be resolved; for example, the appointment of the Children's Guardian; the date by which the adoption agency must submit the Schedule 2 report; and a mutually convenient date for all parties and witnesses to attend the final hearing.

Final hearing You are required to attend this hearing because you are the applicant/s and the court will not hear an application in your absence. You will be represented in court by your solicitor. The judge or magistrates will want to see you in person. If the application is contested, the judge or magistrates will also want to see the birth parents. The judge or magistrate will hear oral evidence and then consider all the circumstances of the case (including the content of the Schedule 2 report) and will decide if the Adoption Order is in the best interests of the child.

Other parties
Local authority If the child is subject to a Care Order or Freeing Order, the local authority is a party to the Adoption Order proceedings. The local authority solicitor and at least the child's social worker (also sometimes a manager or other social work witness) will attend court and participate in the hearing – presenting to the judge the local authority's views on your application.
Birth parents Those with parental responsibility will automatically be parties to the proceedings, and sometimes the court will make a father without parental responsibility a party, and he is then entitled to legal representation in court.
The child Sometimes the court makes a child a party to the proceedings so that he or she can be legally represented. The child's solicitor will usually be instructed by the Children's Guardian. Unless the guardian has asked the court to excuse the child's attendance, he or she will be required to attend court, but only if the judge has decided to dispense with parental agreement and that adoption is in the child's best interests. Therefore the child is not required to attend court to hear the evidence or the legal arguments for and against your application.

Where your identity is not known to the birth parent/s, and if you and the birth parent/s are both attending the final hearing (or any directions hearing), your solicitor should ensure arrangements are made by the court so that you arrive at separate times and do not appear in the courtroom at the same time.

At what age will my child be permitted to read his or her social services records?

Your child may be able to read information held about him or her, or any records, depending on the child's age and level of understanding. Adoption agencies are generally moving towards a more open approach and current practice is certainly to share information. Each case is determined on an individual basis. Of course, your child will not have access to information held about any third party involved. When your child is 18, he or she will be able to access information held about themselves by the agency.

According to the National Adoption Standards:

Children will be well prepared before joining a new family. This will include clear appropriate information on their birth family and life before adoption, and information about the adopters and their family. Children are entitled to information provided by their birth families, which will be kept safe both by agencies and adopters. It will be provided to adopted children, or adults, at a time and in a manner that reflects their age and understanding, as well as the nature of the information concerned.[1]

Are there any records adoptive parents are not entitled to read? If so, why?

You are entitled to read information about yourself that is held by the agency. The agency must also make accessible to you information about your adopted child. However, you are not entitled to read any information about any third parties involved.

The National Adoption Standards say:

Before a match is agreed, adopters will be given full written information to help them understand the needs and background of the child and an opportunity to discuss this and the implications for them and their family.

and

Adoptive parents will be encouraged to keep safe any information provided by birth families via agencies and to provide this to the adopted child on request, or as they feel appropriate.[2]

What is the legal position if I/we decide that we no longer wish to care for a child placed with us by an agency for adoption? Can I/we return the child to the agency?

If you are prospective adopters and the child is living with you *before* an Adoption Order is made, you are not the child's legal parents. You can ask to return the child to the agency, which is obliged to receive the child.

Once an Adoption Order is granted, you, as adoptive parents, become the child's legal parents, and have sole parental responsibility for the child, until and unless a subsequent Adoption Order is granted to other people.

The legal status of an adopted child is the same as a child living with birth parents – the adopted child is regarded in law as having the same status as a child born to the adopters. Once adopted, the child cannot be "returned to the adoption agency", and the adoption agency is not obliged to receive the child into its care.

---

1 Department of Health, *National Adoption Standards for England*, 2001.
2 As above.

However, like any family, you can ask the local authority social services department to assist and advise you in caring for the child, and if you feel you cannot cope with the child at home, you can ask for the child to be accommodated by the local authority. The decision as to whether accommodation is in the best interests of the child rests with the local authority. That accommodation will be in foster care or a children's home for as long as is considered necessary. Like any parents, you will be able to participate in decision-making about your accommodated child, and you may ask for his or her return.

However, if the local authority considers the child to be at risk of significant harm, attributable to the standard of parental care, or that the child is beyond parental control, it may institute court proceedings for an Emergency Protection Order or Care Order.

Helpful resources

Children and Family Courts Advisory and Support Service (CAFCASS)
Practitioners who provide advice to courts about the welfare of children. CAFCASS administers the children's guardians service.
8th floor
Wyndham House
189 Marsh Wall
London E14 9SH
Tel: 020 7510 7000
www.cafcass.co.uk

The Children's Legal Centre
An independent national charity concerned with law and policy affecting children and young people. Produces a monthly journal, *ChildRight*, as well as information sheets and booklets. In addition to policy and campaign work, CLC also provides an advice and information service (free and confidential legal advice); it also has an Education Legal Advocacy Unit, which provides advice and representation to children and/or parents involved in education disputes with a school or local education authority.
The Children's Legal Centre
University of Essex
Wivenhoe Park
Colchester CO4 3SQ
Administration and publications: Tel: 01206 872 466
Essex Children's Project Helpline: Tel: 01206 873 873
Education Law and Advocacy Unit: Tel: 01206 874 807
National Education Law Advice Line: Tel: 0845 345 4345
email: clc@essex.ac.uk
www.childrenslegalcentre.com

Community Legal Service
A government initiative designed to ensure that everyone has access to quality legal advice and information, including by funding legal costs for those on a very low income without significant capital. The service can be provided by Citizens Advice Bureaux (CABs), solicitors' firms and legal advice centres that have been awarded the Community Legal Service Quality mark.

You can find the *Community Legal Service Directory* at your local library. It lists all law firms and advice centres which have the Quality Mark, and indicates whether firms offer free advice or if they charge.

The Community Legal Service website, www.clsdirect.org.uk, provides the Community Legal Service Directory, legal information and advice, and links to websites for other advice organisations.

Tel: 0845 345 4345 for information about CLS providers or about the CLS directory.

Family Rights Group
A national organisation that advises families who are in contact with social services, about the care of their children.
The Print House
18 Ashwin Street
London E8 3DL
Tel: 0800 731 1696
email: office@frg.org.uk
www.frg.org.uk

www.family-solicitors.co.uk
An online information service that provides advice; specific information about adoption; and lists solicitors who specialise in adoption and other aspects of family law.

www.compactlaw.co.uk
An online legal and information service that provides specific information about adoption law.

Money matters

How much does it cost to get an adoption order?

Court fees: These currently range from £30 in the Magistrates Court, to £120 in the County Court and High Court, depending upon the court where the adoption application is filed.

If the child is being adopted from local authority care and the local authority supports the application, the expectation now is that it will pay the court fee.

Legal costs: If the birth parent/s do not agree to, or contest the adoption, you will also be liable for your solicitor's costs in advising and representing you in court. Again, if the child is being adopted from local authority care and the local authority supports the application, it is expected to meet the adopters' legal costs. If you are on income support or a very low income, ask your solicitor about public funding of your legal costs.

Other costs: Adoption agencies can and usually do charge a fee for an assessment of prospective adopters of children from overseas. If you are adopting from overseas, you will also incur travel expenses and may have to pay additional fees to authorities in the child's country of origin (see Section 1 for more details).

What types of financial assistance may be available to help with our adopted child?

For children adopted from care, financial help may be available during placement of the child and before the Adoption Order is granted.

Different types of financial support may be available to prospective adoptive parents. This support is based upon the financial need of the adoptive family and upon the particular costs the family will incur as a result of being introduced to the child, and the child going to live with them. Each local authority will assess the family's need in order to determine if support is necessary. The types of support *may* include:

- travel expenses for introductions to the child;

- travel expenses for the child's contact with his or her birth family;

- costs of beds, wardrobes, etc. (for example, if you are adopting a sibling group);

- special equipment and house adaptations;

- payment for loss or damage;

- a maintenance allowance, payable weekly or monthly by the local authority, until the Adoption Order is applied for or granted – this usually is at the same or lower rate than a fostering allowance, on a scale that increases with the child's age;

- other financial support that might include respite care, emergency support, domestic help, therapy for the child, or other costs involved during the placement.

If the child is less than five years old, placed singly and without significant special needs or disabilities, it is unlikely that most of these expenses will be met by local authorities or that a maintenance allowance will be paid.

State benefits for a child's special needs (such as Disability Living Allowance or Invalid Care Allowance) are unlikely to be available to adopters until after the Adoption Order is granted. Child benefit is payable from the date of placement for adoption.

Is regular financial support available after an adoption order?

Regular financial support can be paid on a weekly or monthly basis to adoptive parents after the Adoption Order is granted. This allowance is permitted under the Adoption Act 1976 and the Adoption Support Services (Local Authorities) (England) Regulations 2003 (and equivalent regulations in Wales). Financial support is designed to facilitate adoptions of children who might otherwise not be adopted, due to the financial cost to the adopters. The allowance is not taxable.

According to the Adoption Support Services Regulations 2003, financial support may be paid if one or more of the following circumstances exist:

- the child has not been placed with the adoptive parents for adoption, and financial support is necessary to ensure that the adoptive parents can look after the child if placed with them;

- the child has been placed with the adoptive parents for adoption, and financial support is necessary to ensure that the adoptive parents can continue to look after the child;

- the child has been adopted, and financial support is necessary to ensure that the adoptive parents can continue to look after the child;

- the local authority is satisfied that the child has established a strong and important relationship with the adoptive parent before the adoption order is made;

- it is desirable that the child be placed with the same adoptive parents as his or her brother or sister (whether of the full blood or half blood), or with a child with whom he or she has previously shared a home;

- the child needs special care which requires a greater expenditure of resources by reason of illness, disability, emotional or behavioural difficulties or the continuing consequences of past abuse or neglect;

- on account of the age, sex or ethnic origin of the child it is necessary for the local authority to make special arrangements to facilitate the placement of the child for adoption.

The amount payable as regular financial support is determined by the local authority, which takes into account the adopters' financial resources and commitments.

Allowances paid after adoption must not include any element of fee or reward. However, the exception to this is when foster carers wish to adopt a child whom they are fostering. They may continue to receive an allowance which includes a reward element for two years and, in some situations, for longer, after an Adoption Order.

Adopters receiving an allowance must inform the local authority of changes in their financial or other circumstances and supply an annual statement of their finances. Allowances must be reviewed annually.

Payment of an allowance may affect other benefits you receive, such as Income Support. Contact the Benefit Enquiry Line (0800 220 674) for more information.

What about a lump-sum payment?

Instead of a regular ongoing allowance the local authority may agree with you to pay you a single lump-sum payment or a series of lump-sum payments, to meet a specific assessed need.

Can I apply for financial support after an Adoption Order?

Yes. The Adoption Support Services Regulations 2003 provide that adoptive families can ask for their need for adoption support, including financial support, to be assessed at any point after an Adoption Order until their child is 18. Local authorities have a duty to do an assessment if asked. You would need to apply to the local authority which placed the child with you unless it is more than three years since the child was placed and more than a year since the Adoption Order, whichever is longer. If this is the case, you need to apply to the local authority where you live.

Taking action ...

... to understand your entitlements regarding financial support

There is currently a lack of consistency among local authorities in assessment and payment of allowances.

However, local authorities are *required* to:

1 consider if an allowance should be paid

2 inform adopters about available allowances

3 give adopters written notice of the proposed decision about adoption allowance

4 hear representation from adopters about allowances

5 review the allowance annually.

If you believe your needs have not been fairly assessed or if you have other complaints about the adoption allowance, use your local authority complaints procedure in the first instance. If you still are not satisfied, you may contact your Local Authority Ombudsman.

Local authorities may not be forthright about publicising available allowances. The National Adoption Standards will require local authorities to make this explicit: 'Councils, with the relevant agencies ... will provide or commission a comprehensive range of pre- and post-adoption services consistent with any national framework or regulation. These will facilitate and support adoption, and meet the needs of children who move between local authority areas. *Criteria for access to services will be clear, concise and understandable.*'[3]

3 Department of Health, *National Adoption Standards for England*, 2001.

Other benefits

Other types of benefits may be payable to adoptive parents by the Benefits Agency, as for any child in their family, under certain circumstances. These benefits are not automatically payable if you have an adopted child with physical, mental or emotional difficulties. However, it is worth knowing which benefits exist and are available in case you require financial support at some point in the life of your adopted child. You will need to find out which are means tested. These benefits currently include:

Disability Living Allowance (DLA) Some families now receive DLA for children who have attachment difficulties. This is the exception, not the rule, however, and you will have to apply to your local benefits office in order to receive this payment.

Carer's Allowance Adoptive parents, like all parents of children with disabilities, may be eligible for Carer's Allowance *in addition* to Disability Living Allowance, as long as one parent is not in full-time employment or earning more than £50 per week (irrespective of the partner's income). Many adoptive parents (usually mothers) are unable to take jobs because the needs of their children are so immense and because childcare arrangements are generally unable to meet the children's specific needs.

Helpful resources

For information about benefits, contact:

- Benefit Enquiry Line 0800 220 674

- your local post office (applications and information about various available benefits)

- your local Citizens Advice Bureau (offers advice and information) – check your local phone book for the Bureau nearest you

- your local authority's welfare rights department (usually located within social services)

Am I entitled to leave during the adoption of my child?

Yes – both statutory adoption leave and pay and also statutory paternity leave and pay are now available (see section 1).

Taking action ...

... benefits provisions of the Carers and Disabled Children Act 2000

If your child has a physical or mental disability as defined by this Act, then you or your child may be eligible for:

- direct payments to 16- and 17-year-old young people who have a disability

- direct payments to carers to meet their own assessed needs – this may mean that parents of a disabled child could receive a direct payment, rather than use the services provided by the local council, perhaps because they think existing services are not suitable or appropriate for their child.

Contact your local Benefits Agency for more information about this benefit and see Section 4.

schooling and education

3

In this section

- gain a general overview of the types of problems some adopted children may have in school

- learn how schools can meet the needs of children who have difficulties

- understand the process of obtaining special educational provision for your child

- find out about current government initiatives and regulations to help you understand what support and services your child may be entitled to at school

- find organisations and resources that can help you support your child at school and help you obtain the services that meet his or her specific needs

3 schooling and education

Helpful resources

... to inform staff about the impact of emotional trauma on a child's ability to learn:

Learn the Child: Helping looked after children to learn, by Kate Cairns and Chris Stanway, BAAF, 2004. Good practice guide on helping and supporting traumatised children and young people in their learning.

'The effects of trauma on childhood learning', by Kate Cairns. Describes the impact of trauma on the body and brain and suggests ways in which children can be helped to learn. It is included in the anthology, ***Nobody Ever Told Us School Mattered***, edited by Sonia Jackson, BAAF, 2001.

GOING TO SCHOOL is one of the main activities of childhood. Schooling not only teaches children academic skills, but also provides essential lessons in identity formation, relationship building and socialisation. Many adopted and fostered children have **learning difficulties** that may affect their ability to learn and/or their ability to socialise successfully with other children. According to the Department for Education and Skills (DfES), previously the Department for Education and Employment (DfEE), 'learning difficulty' means that '... the child has significantly greater difficulty in learning than most children of the same age; or the child has a disability which needs different educational facilities from those that schools generally provide for children of the same age in the area'.[1]

Learning difficulties include apparent physical disabilities (such as motor disabilities, deafness or blindness) as well as less apparent difficulties, such as dyslexia, slow learners or "emotionally vulnerable" children.

In some cases, "emotionally vulnerable" children may be identified as having an "**emotional/behavioural difficulty**" (EBD). This is defined by the SEN (Special Educational Needs) Code of Practice (see p.59) as 'a learning difficulty that requires special education provision'.

Some children may not be officially "identified" as having either of these difficulties, but may nevertheless have problems with academic and/or social skills at school.

It is important that adoptive parents recognise the possibility that their children may have difficulty at school. Your child will benefit if you are observant of his or her schoolwork and behaviour, and communicate openly with school staff. At the same time, it is also important to try to keep a "balanced" view of "normal" childhood behaviours and social interactions at school.

What are we entitled to know about our child's educational history?

The Children Act 1989 requires local authorities to provide a Care Plan for every child in its care. The Care Plan should '... take account of the child's educational history, the need to achieve continuity, and the need to identify any educational need which the child may have, or carry out any assessment in respect of any special educational need'. Within the Care Plan, local authorities are required (according to Local Authority Circular (2000) 13) to provide a Personal Education Plan (PEP) that '...ensures access to services and support; contributes to stability, minimises disruption and broken schooling; signals particular and special needs; establishes clear goals and acts as a record of progress and achievement'. The plan should:

- provide an achievement record (academic and otherwise);

- identify short-term targets; and

- establish long-term plans and aspirations.

1 Previously available on www.dfee.gov.uk/sen/sengloss, 2001, p.52.

Helpful resources

What Does Adoption Mean for Today's Children? A guide for teachers a 5-page leaflet with general information and tips for teachers. Available from Adoption UK.

Government guidance also recommends that schools provide a "designated teacher" who oversees the education of children in care. However, this guidance is not law, so services may vary among education authorities.

To help ensure continuity in meeting your child's educational needs after placement with you:

- ask to review copies of your child's Care Plan and PEP;

- speak to your child's teachers and/or designated teacher within his or her current school; and share the PEP and other relevant information with new teachers, if your child is moving to a new school.

For more information, contact the DfES or access the Guidance on the Education of Children and Young People in Public Care on www.dfes.gov.uk/incare.

The following guidance for social workers from BAAF outlines the details you should be informed about when considering your child's educational background and current needs.

… families need to be fully aware of the child's educational history and [to] have the opportunity to discuss this with appropriate professionals, and … to read and discuss educational assessments and statements … formal liaison between education departments is crucial to ensuring that the necessary … information is exchanged and that, with the family's involvement, the most suitable school can be identified … Social workers have important roles to play in co-ordinating the efforts of all involved to meet the individual needs of both child and family.[2]

Should I tell the school/teachers about my child's background?

Whether or not you choose to share details of your child's background with school staff is entirely your own choice. Some parents may fear that their child will be treated "differently" if teachers know he or she is adopted, or that other children will ostracise the child if they discover anything about that child's background.

You might find that sharing selected details with school staff will help them treat your child appropriately during certain portions of the school curriculum – such as studying family history or family trees.

If your child has significant academic or socialisation problems that affect his or her schooling, then you will most likely have to share some details of adoption with school staff. Often, open communication with teachers will help them work with your child in an appropriate and helpful manner.

2 S. Byrne, *Linking and Introductions*, BAAF, 2000, p.13.

Terms you may need to know

Independent School A school neither maintained by a local education authority (LEA), nor a grant maintained school, but is registered under the Education Act 1944. Section 189 of the Education Act 1993 gives the conditions under which an independent school may be approved by the Secretary of State as being suitable for the admission of children with statements of Special Educational Needs (see www.dfes.gov.uk, 2001).

Individual Education Plan (IEP) A written document, prepared by school staff, which lists specific goals a child should aim to achieve during a named school term. The goals in an IEP can include educational achievements, as well as improvements in social skills. Parents and older children can participate in writing the IEP.

Learning Support Unit (LSU) A classroom provided to support persistently disruptive, violent or unco-operative pupils. The LSU may offer an alternative curriculum and may also offer individual counselling. The goal of the LSU is to enable students to return to the mainstream school, if possible.

Learning Support Assistant (LSA) A person who helps children who are in mainstream school, but who require extra learning support. LSAs are not specially trained, but are supported by the teacher and sometimes by visiting specialists.

Named LEA Officer The person from the LEA who liaises with parents about arrangements concerning their child's assessment and statementing process. The LEA will inform parents of the Named Officer when it proposes to conduct a statutory assessment of the child.

Named Person A person whom the LEA *must* identify when it sends parents a final version of their child's Statement of Special Educational Needs. (Ideally, this person may be appointed at the beginning of the assessment process so he or she can attend meetings with parents and can encourage parents to participate in the process.) The Named Person must be someone who can give the parents information and advice about their child's special educational needs. The Named Person should be independent of the LEA and may be someone from a voluntary organisation or a parent partnership scheme (see p.60 and *Helpful resources*, pp.61-2).

Non-maintained special school Schools in England approved by the Secretary of State as special schools which are not maintained by the state, but charge fees on a non-profit-making basis. Most non-maintained special schools are run by major charities or charitable trusts (see www.dfes.gov.uk, 2001).

Special Educational Needs Co-ordinator (SENCo)
A teacher, appointed by the head teacher, who co-ordinates the services required for all children in the school who have special educational needs. This person can serve as a liaison between parents and the LEA.

Special school 'A school which is specially organised to make special educational provision for pupils with special educational needs and is, for the time being, approved by the Secretary of State under section 188 of the Education Act 1993' (see www.dfes.gov.uk, 2001).

Statement of Special Educational Needs A written document that is prepared by the LEA after assessing a child. The document outlines, in detail, the child's educational needs and proposes how those needs should be met (see p.59). LEAs must review the statement every 12 months.

How do I choose a good school for my child?

In addition to the usual considerations you have when choosing a school for your child, you also may have to think about the following questions if your child has learning and/or emotional/behavioural difficulties:

- Does this school have experience of dealing with learning difficulties or emotional/behavioural difficulties?

- Does this school have the physical and/or financial resources needed to address learning or emotional/behavioural difficulties?

- Does the school specifically state it can handle emotional/behavioural difficulties?

- Can I communicate easily and comfortably with teachers and with the head teacher?

- How large is the school? Smaller class size and higher teacher to student ratios may make a smaller school easier for some adopted children. A small school, however, may not have the financial and/or physical resources that your child might require.

Independent schools are not subject to LEA regulations regarding special educational needs (see below) as are state-supported schools. You may find that some independent schools offer specific resources for children with "special needs". You should ask the school for its definition of "special needs" – sometimes these are defined only as learning difficulties and do not include emotional/behavioural difficulties.

What are "special educational needs"?

"Special educational needs" (SEN) include a broad range of problems that affect children at school – from specific learning difficulties to emotional/ behavioural problems and developmental problems. The Department for Education and Skills (DfES) provides the following definition for special educational needs:

A child is defined as having special educational needs if he or she has a learning difficulty which needs special teaching. A learning difficulty means that the child has significantly greater difficulty in learning than most children of the same age. Or, it means a child has a disability which needs different educational facilities from those that schools generally provide for children of the same age in the area. The children who need special … education are not only those with obvious learning difficulties … [but also] those whose learning difficulties are less apparent, such as slow learners and emotionally vulnerable children.[3]

An official definition of SEN is provided by the Code of Practice (1994) of the Education Act 1993. Identifying and addressing Special Educational Needs should occur in three distinct phases, according to the Code of Practice:

1 Using existing school resources: if your child has difficulty at school, for example, difficulty following instructions, paying attention, or writing down information, the Code of Practice requires the school to address the problem using its existing resources, such as a classroom assistant or different teaching strategies.

2 If your child does not make progress, despite the support received from school, the school can consult external services (within education or other services) for specialist strategies or materials.

3 DfES, Parents' Centre, www.dfes.gov.uk, 2001.

The National Advisory Group on Special Educational Needs was established in 1997 to advise the government about SEN issues. The **Emotional and Behavioural Difficulties Sub-group** prepared an advisory report for the government, entitled *Developing a National Policy for Children with Emotional and Behavioural Difficulties*. Details of this report are available from the DfES or from its website (see *Helpful resources*, p.62).

The Government has implemented The Schools Access Initiative to provide funds to improve access to mainstream schools for children with learning difficulties. For details about this initiative, see the Government's White Paper, *Valuing People: A new strategy for learning disability*. The report costs £15.90 from HMSO (see Appendix 2) or is available on the internet at www.dh.gov.uk.

3   If progress is not made, then your child is entitled to a statutory assessment of SEN by your LEA. This usually involves your child completing a series of tests administered by the LEA's educational psychologist. The LEA must comply with a request for an assessment unless it has already assessed the child within the last six months or if it decides an assessment is not necessary. Parents can appeal against this decision.

The LEA is required to provide a **Statement of Special Educational Needs** for your child if:

- your child would be best served in a different mainstream school or by specialist resources within the same school; or

- your child would benefit from specialist and frequent support; daily LSA support; special equipment; regular involvement of non-educational agencies; or placement in a day or residential special school.

If your child is assessed for a statement, it does not necessarily mean that the LEA will issue a statement. For example, the LEA may find that your child's needs can be met within existing school resources. The LEA must then issue a "note in lieu" to the parents and must also inform parents of their right to appeal this decision.

Each LEA is now also required to inform parents of its **"parent partnership" service**, in which a "named person" is identified to support parents whose child is undergoing the statementing process. Each LEA should have a named **LEA officer** who liaises with parents about statutory assessment and preparing a statement.

If your child receives a Statement of Special Educational Needs, the statement must be reviewed every year by you, the head teacher, an LEA representative and any other person involved with your child at school. Older children may also participate in these meetings.

The current trend among education authorities in England and Wales is to educate children in mainstream schools whenever possible; to work co-operatively with other agencies and services (e.g. health and social services); to meet students' special needs; and to implement creative and cost-effective ways to address special educational needs within schools. At the moment, services for children with special educational needs vary widely among education authorities. If your child requires SEN services, therefore, you may have to communicate openly and frequently with your school and with your LEA to help your child obtain the services that will best meet his or her educational needs.

It may sometimes seem like you have to dig through endless layers of bureaucracy in order to obtain the services that will best meet your child's needs. But keep digging – it is the best way to make sure that the school and the LEA understand your child's needs and provide the resources required. It may also help pave the way for other adoptive families dealing with the school system.

Taking action ...

... to understand your child's entitlements to special education provision

SEN Code of Practice (2001) – provides schools and LEAs with a framework for making decisions about various aspects of special educational needs – it provides general guidance, but does not dictate what LEAs must do in individual cases. The Code of Practice has recently been revised, based on consultation with the National Advisory Group on SEN, and came into force on 1 January 2002. The revised code gives a brief definition of "emotional/behavioural difficulties" and provides extra detail in Government Circular 9/94. Technically speaking, government circulars provide "guidance" and are not law, so parents should be aware that LEAs and/or SEN Tribunals are not required by law to follow such guidance.

SEN Tribunal – a judicial body to which parents can appeal for any of the following reasons:

i) if the LEA decides not to assess their child for SEN;

ii) if the LEA assesses the child, but decides not to issue a statement of special educational needs;

iii) if parents disagree with the LEA's decision about what SEN help the child needs;

iv) or if the LEA tries to withdraw the child's statement, but the parents think the child still needs it.

The Tribunal's decision is binding on the LEA, regardless of the cost or resources required to meet the child's needs. The SEN Tribunal is required to follow the SEN Code of Practice when making its decisions.

Government Circular 01/98 – This circular is entitled *Coverage of Behaviour Support Plans* and includes general guidance to LEAs about providing support and assistance in schools for pupils with emotional/behavioural difficulties. LEAs are not required to follow this guidance, because it is not law. However, this information can give parents a general idea of the types of services the LEA is expected to provide.

Helpful resources

Contact your LEA or county council to find out if it produces a Parents' Information Guide about schools in your area and their services, including special educational needs. Some LEAs or councils, such as Warwickshire, also have a website that provides such information. Search on www.dfes.gov.uk/info/dfeelen.htm to find out if a site exists for your local area.

Organisations

Advisory Centre for Education (ACE)

Provides information about all aspects of state education, and helps parents who are dealing with schools or education authorities.

Unit 1C
Aberdeen Studios
22 Highbury Grove
London N5 2EA
Tel: 0808 800 5793 (advice line 2–5pm)
"Exclusion" advice line 0808 800 0327
www.ace-ed.org.uk

British Institute for Learning Disabilities (BILD)

An independent, registered charity founded in 1972 to improve the quality of life for all people who have a learning disability. The institute conducts research into various aspects of learning disabilities, and provides information and services for people with learning disabilities,

their families and for the professional community.
Campion House, Green Street
Kidderminster
Worcestershire DY10 1JL
Tel: 01562 723 010
email: enquiries@bild.org.uk
www.bild.org.uk

Caspari Foundation (formerly Forum for Educational Therapy and Therapeutic Teaching, FAETT)

Established in 2000, this organisation promotes educational therapy and therapeutic learning to help children who have emotional barriers that can impair learning. Provides courses for teachers, as well as consultations for children and their parents.
Caspari House
1 Noel Road
London N1 8HQ
Tel: 020 7704 1977
email: admin@caspari.org.uk
www.caspari.org.uk

Children in Scotland

Provides a national information and advice service, *Enquire*, for parents, professionals, children and young people living in Scotland who have questions about special educational needs. Also operates a telephone helpline, training events, written information and four mediation projects.

5 Shandwick Place
Edinburgh EH2 4RG
Helpline: 0845 123 2303
email: enquire.seninfo@childreninscotland.org.uk
www.childreninscotland.org.uk

Children's Legal Centre, Education and Advocacy Unit

Provides advice and representation to children and/or parents involved in education disputes with a school or a local education authority. The Unit operates within the south-east of England. For education disputes outside this area, the Centre can provide advice, as well as negotiation and mediation services.
University of Essex
Wivenhoe Park
Colchester CO4 3SQ
Tel: 0845 345 4345
www.childrenslegalcentre.com

Department for Education and Skills (DfES)

Provides information for parents about all aspects of education and schools. The DfES website offers a Parents' Centre that provides specific and comprehensive information about SEN. Contact the DfES publications department to find out about specific information for parents, such as the SEN Guide for Parents, and for a copy of the Code of Practice.
DfES Publications
PO Box 5050
Annesley
Nottingham NG15 0DL
Tel: 0845 602 2260
Fax: 0845 603 3360
email: dfes@prolog.uk.com
www.parentcentre.gov.uk

Independent Panel for Special Education Advice (IPSEA)

A volunteer-based organisation that aims to ensure that children with special educational needs receive the special education provision to which they are legally entitled. Provides free, independent advice; free advice on appealing to the Special Educational Needs Tribunal (including representation, if needed); second opinions from professionals.
6 Carlow Mews
Woodbridge
Suffolk IP12 1EA

Advice line: Tel: 0800 018 4016 or 01394 380 518
Scotland: Tel: 0131 665 4396
Northern Ireland: Tel: 01232 705 654
Tribunal appeals only: Tel: 01394 384 711
www.ipsea.org.uk

The Institute for Arts in Therapy and Education

A college of higher education dedicated to in-depth theoretical and practical study of artistic, imaginative and emotional expression, and to the understanding and enhancement of emotional well-being.
2 – 18 Britannia Row
London N1 8PA
Tel: 020 7704 2534
www.artspsychotherapy.co.uk

National Association for Special Educational Needs (NASEN)

Promotes the education, training, advancement and development of people with special educational needs. Services to members include several regular publications, and regional courses and conferences.
4 – 5 Amber Business Village
Amber Close, Amington
Tamworth
Staffs B77 4RP
Tel: 01827 311 500
email: welcom@nasen.org.uk
www.nasen.org.uk

Warwickshire Parent Partnership Service

LEAs are required to provide a Parent Partnership Service (PPS). It provides support for parents of children with special educational needs, via telephone contact, home visits or school meetings. PPS staff liaise with schools, LEA officers and Special Educational Needs Support Services. The Service organises regular meetings for parents and offers workshops to schools and governors, and to health and social services providers. Contact the National Parent Partnership Network for information about your local service.
c/o ContinYou
Unit C1, Grovelands Court
Grovelands Estate
Lonford Road
Exhall
Coventry CV7 9NE
Tel: 024 7658 8440
email: pps@cedc.org.uk

School Health Service

Identifies and assesses children who have physical, emotional or behavioural problems. It includes a named school nurse and paediatric doctors who have additional training to help with school services. The Health Service provides advice to LEAs and offers specialist services, such as enuresis (bedwetting) clinics, audiology services, and support/advice for families and children with physical and emotional difficulties. Contact your local authority or LEA to find phone numbers for your local School Health Teams.

Special Education Consortium

c/o Council for Disabled Children
8 Wakley Street
London EC1V 7QE
Tel: 020 7843 1900
email: sportic@ncb.org.uk
www.ncb.org.uk/cdc/sec.htm

Information about learning difficulties

DDAT (UK) Ltd

Provides assessment, consultation and treatment for children, adolescents and adults who may have dyslexia, dyspraxia or attention difficulties. Contact the Centre for further information about its services and its fees.
Camden House
Warwick Road
Kenilworth CV8 1TH
Tel: 0870 737 0011/0870 880 6060
email: info@ddat.co.uk
www.ddat.co.uk

The Institute for Neuro-phsyiological Psychology

Established in 1975 to research the effects of central nervous system dysfunction on learning difficulties in children and on adults suffering from neuroses. The institute provides detailed information about this topic and about its services on its website or via post. Contact the institute for further information about its services and its fees.
Warwick House
1 Stanley Street
Chester CH1 2LR
Tel: 01244 311 414
www.inpp.org.uk

The Mental Health Foundation

Provides information and support for people and families who have any type of mental health problem and/or learning disability. Included within the MHF is The Foundation for People with Learning Disabilities.
7th Floor, 83 Victoria Street
London SW1H 0HW
Tel: 020 7802 0300
email: mhf@mhf.org.uk
www.mentalhealth.org.uk

Scotland office:
5th Floor, Merchants House
30 George Square
Glasgow G2 1EG
email: scotland@mhf.org.uk
www.mentalhealth.org.uk
www.learningdisabilities.org.uk

Information about home schooling

Home Education Advisory Service (HEAS)

A UK-based national charity providing information and support for home education. Produces information, provides support for parents, works with LEAs to monitor and inspect home education programmes.
PO Box 98
Welwyn Garden City
Hertfordshire AL8 6AN
Tel: 01707 371 854
email: admin@heas.org.uk
www.heas.org.uk

Publications

Banished to the Exclusion Zone: School exclusion and the law
Available from the Children's Legal Centre.
See Appendix 2 for contact details.

Behind the Behaviour
A new video to help teachers understand the role they can play in children's mental health.
Available from Mental Health Media
Tel: 020 7700 8171

Learning Disabilities in Children by Peter Burke and Katy Cigno, Blackwell Science, 2000.
Explains how learning difficulties are defined and examines their impact on family life. The book is aimed at those working in child welfare, social work and community care.

***Learn the Child: Helping looked after children to
learn*** by Kate Cairns and Chris Stanway, BAAF, 2004.
A training resource for social workers, carers and teachers
on helping looked after children to learn. It could also be
helpful to adoptive parents.

The Mental Health Needs of Looked After Children
edited by Joanna Richardson and Carol Joughin, Gaskell,
2000.
Presents information on a range of mental health issues
affecting children in care. Incorporates opinions and
perspectives of children in the care system, and includes
professional information and guidance regarding the
young people's views.

***Nobody Ever Told Us School Mattered: Raising the
educational attainments of children in care***
edited by Sonia Jackson, BAAF, 2001.
An anthology that considers what can be done to ensure
that looked after children have a better chance to succeed.

***Promoting Children's Mental Health within Early
Years and School Settings***
A booklet produced by the Department for Education and
Skills (DfES) to help teachers and other people working
co-operatively with health professionals, to promote
children's mental health. It provides examples of mental
health initiatives taking place within schools and gives
advice on how to help children who are having difficulties
or who have defined mental health problems.
DfES Publications
PO Box 5050, Sherwood Park, Annesley
Nottingham NG15 0DJ
Tel: 0845 602 2260
Quote reference number: 0112/2001

***Special Education Handbook: The law on children
with special needs***
Explains the process of obtaining a statement of special

educational needs and various aspects of the
statementing process.
Available from the Advisory Centre for Education (see
p.61).

Special Educational Needs: A guide for parents
Available free from the Department for Education and
Skills (DfES) publications section (see p.62).

Special Educational Needs Update
A newsletter published by the DfES and sent to all
schools, local education authorities, health authorities,
social services departments, and NHS Trusts in England.
For more information contact the DfES.
Tel: 0845 602 2260
www.dfes/gov/sen/update.

***Special Needs: A guide for parents and carers of
Jewish children with special educational needs***
Available from the Board of Deputies of British Jews
Tel: 020 7543 5400

Special Schools in Britain 2000 – 2001
published by NASEN (see p.62).

Websites

Center for Positive Behavioral Intervention and Support
www.pbis.org
Created by the US Department of Education to help
schools implement and sustain positive behaviour-
intervention programmes.

Department for Education and Skills (DfES) Standards website
www.standards.dfes.gov.uk
Provides links to various government initiatives for
raising standards in education, and provides a database
of good practice programmes throughout the country.

your child: physical and emotional needs

4

In this section

- learn about the general effects of trauma and neglect on children

- examine the emotional and physical difficulties adopted children may experience

- find out how to access the services your child may need and how to ensure your child receives the help to which he or she is entitled

- gather information about the organisations and resources which can help you and your child with particular difficulties

CHILDREN IN NEED OF ADOPTION OR FOSTERING will have experienced separation from their birth families. These children, *regardless of their age*, will be affected (to varying degrees) by that separation. In addition to the effects of separation and loss, many of these children may also have experienced varying degrees of trauma as a result of neglect and/or abuse.

Many of us are generally familiar with the *physical* impact of neglect and abuse on children. However, it is important to be aware that the *emotional* effects of early trauma may be less obvious, but equally profound. The repercussions of this trauma can deeply affect your child, no matter at what age you adopted him or her.

Today there are many resources and services to help children who have physical, emotional and developmental difficulties as a result of early trauma. The purpose of this section, therefore, is to give you a basic understanding of the possible needs your adopted child may have, so that you can find the services and information to meet your child's needs.

Varying degrees ... what does it mean?

The phrase, "varying degrees", applies to all of the problems discussed in this section. Every child is an individual and your adopted child may – or may not – experience the difficulties presented here. There are many factors that determine how extensively a child is affected by emotional or physical trauma. These include the age of the child when he or she experienced the trauma and the length of time the child experienced the trauma. Younger children are less likely to be affected as deeply as older children – but even children adopted as infants can show the effects of early trauma later in life.

It may be difficult for you – or for the professionals involved with your adoption – to determine exactly how much your child may be affected by past experiences and what needs your child may have now or in the future. But you will be able to help yourself and your child, if you are aware of potential difficulties that may arise, and know where to seek appropriate help if you need it.

Possible effects of neglect and/or abuse in children

ABUSE AND NEGLECT OF CHILDREN can take several forms. The word "abuse" commonly refers to a clearly identifiable event or series of events in a child's life, whereas "neglect" refers to an ongoing experience of deprivation. "Abuse", however, can sometimes be used to cover both situations, so it is important to be clear about what has actually happened to a child. A common image of children in the care system is of children who have been sexually or physically abused. Yet many of them are being looked after solely as a result of neglect of their basic needs and such neglect can sometimes damage a child more than individual episodes of abuse.[1]

Regardless of how it occurs, neglect and abuse are **traumatic events** for a child. You may often hear health professionals refer to children experiencing trauma or being traumatised – a word defined in medical circles as meaning 'an emotionally painful and harmful event that sometimes leads to long-term mental difficulties'. It is this trauma that creates the emotional wounds that may take many years (or even a lifetime) to resolve.

What information can I find from the child's medical records?

Your child's social worker is required by law to give you full information in writing about your child when the agency has agreed to his or her placement with you. This is usually recorded on BAAF's health assessment forms. These include *Form IHA-C* (Initial Health Assessment Child) or *Form IHA-YP* (Initial Health Assessment Young Person), depending on the age of the young person, and this assessment should be regularly reviewed and recorded on BAAF's *Form RHA-C* (Review Health Assessment Child) or *Form RHA-YP* (Review Health Assessment Young Person). Two other forms, *Annexe to Form C* (profile of behavioural and emotional well-being of a child aged 1 to 5), and *Annexe to Form D* (profile of behavioural and emotional well-being of a child aged between 5 and 10), are used to record behavioural and emotional development. The initial health assessment of your child will record physical and mental development, and will also indicate any issues that should be followed up. A copy of the health assessment report will be sent to your child's GP as well as to you. It is sensible to discuss this either with your GP or with the agency's medical adviser, who may have carried out the assessment and who will in any case submit comments on it to the adoption court. The making of an Adoption Order does not prevent you from consulting your adoption agency and its medical adviser if you have any concerns about your child's health. You may also ask your GP to consult the agency on your behalf.

1 See D. Goldman, *Emotional Intelligence: Why it can matter more than IQ*, New York, Bantam Books, 1997, p.195.

Your child's health assessment may include information about his or her birth parents. It is important to remember that this information, whether given or implied, must be treated as strictly confidential, privy only to yourselves as parents, to your child's GP, to the adoption court and, when he or she is older, to your child.

What physical and/or developmental problems might we have to deal with?

Symptoms of neglect or abuse can include, for example, severe nappy rash, inadequate and unexplained weight gain or loss, withdrawn behaviour (or its opposite, indiscriminate displays of affection), unexplained bruises and a history of frequent visits to hospital accident and emergency departments. Health visitors, doctors, social workers, teachers, and others involved with the child can initiate action on the child's behalf to deal with the situation, which for some children may include being looked after by the local authority. A child's physical and emotional development will often improve with placement in a secure and loving environment, although in many cases this will take months, or even longer.

There may be some physical and developmental problems which do *not* go away after the child is placed with you or which may take many years to overcome. Some of these difficulties, such as small size, can result from poor antenatal care, as well as neglect after the child is born. These are difficulties, therefore, that you may have to deal with as adoptive parents.

Physical problems In addition to any diagnosed conditions the child might have been born with (e.g. Down's syndrome, asthma, other physical disabilities), the child may have general problems, such as small size (height and weight) for his or her age and a tendency to contract minor illnesses (such as colds or other types of infections) more frequently than other children. Some children may have problems with wetting and soiling (day and/or night), due to delayed physical development. It will be important for you to work closely with your health visitor and/or GP to help your child with these problems. Although these problems will improve over time, your child may never completely overcome some of them.

Possible developmental delays due to neglect

- delayed language skills
- limited attention span
- delayed motor skills
- learning difficulties
- immature behaviour for his or her age
- immature behaviour when interacting with other children
- lack of self-esteem
- inability to control emotions (anger and joy)

Developmental problems Children who have been neglected do not develop the same "skills" as other children of their age. Neglected children, for example, may not learn how to talk or how to speak properly; they may be slow in learning how to walk or run, how to throw a ball, how to use the toilet, or how to eat properly. These are only a few of the skills a neglected child may not learn. The extent to which a child develops skills will differ with each individual and will also depend on the extent and time-scale of the neglect.

2 S. Byrne, *Linking and Introductions*, BAAF, 2000, p.13.

Chicken or egg ...?

It may be difficult to determine whether or not a child's difficulties are caused by physical, developmental or emotional problems. If your eight-year-old son wets himself at school, for example, is this problem due to a delay in his bladder development, delayed emotional maturity, distraction by other people at school, or the distance he has to travel to use the school toilets? Sometimes, all of these factors contribute to a child's

problems. Thus, many parents don't know where to look for help.

A good place to begin looking for help is from your GP and/or health visitor. Ask for information about the Child Development Clinic in your area and/or the local paediatric consultant. You can also contact your local Health Authority for information about Child Development Services in your area (see *Taking Action*, below).

Taking action ...

... to obtain health services for your child

Health services for babies, children and adolescents are provided by a range of professionals in both hospital and the community. The health visitor has a helpful role in health promotion and in identifying the health care needs of under-fives and in helping to ensure access to the services necessary to meet those needs. Health authorities/boards are obliged, under Section 10 of the Education Act 1981, to inform parents of children under 5 of any relevant voluntary organisation which could help with a childhood disability or learning difficulty. This means that health authorities should keep information about local self-help groups etc. in order to provide effective information services.

Every child born since 1992 has a **Personal Child Health Record** – make sure you obtain this from your social worker or voluntary agency. If this record cannot be located, ask your local health visitor or GP to arrange for a new one to be made for your child. There are often delays in securing health records of children who have had several moves from area to area or who have a complicated medical history including hospital treatment. You may need to encourage your GP or hospital to persist in chasing these records. Sometimes the child's change of name presents a barrier to be negotiated, and your adoption agency's medical adviser should be able to help you with this.

Children's Health Charter – this was part of the Patient's Charter and set out the standards of services that children and young people could expect in the NHS. It still applies in Wales, Scotland and Northern Ireland but, in

England, it has been superseded by the NHS Plan (see below).

The Children's Taskforce – The NHS Plan, published in July 2000, set out a radical programme of reform for the NHS and social care service. The Children's Taskforce is one of ten Taskforces that were established to turn that Plan into a reality. Its mission is: 'To secure the health and well-being of all children throughout childhood and into adult life'. The Taskforce exists to make sure that the NHS plan delivers real improvements for children, young people, and their families. It has launched several projects, including some that address health needs; children and adolescent mental health services; improving the life chances of looked after children; safeguarding children; and bringing together services to disabled children across both health and social services.

Community Health Services for Children – these services can include: audiology, child development assistance, occupational therapy, physiotherapy, school health services, services for children with a learning disability, and speech and language therapy, in addition to other services. Services may include a **Learning Disability Nursing Team** – nurses with specialist training to work with children who have a learning disability. They can provide help, support and advice, such as developing relationship and life skills, continence, physical or sensory disabilities. Contact your GP or your local health authority for details of this service in your area.

Health Link Worker (usually a named health visitor or named school health adviser) can co-ordinate services needed by pre-school and school-aged children who require extra health care.

Most children learn many of these skills and, with time, catch up to their age level when they are placed in a nurturing environment. If you are unsure of your child's physical and/or developmental status when he or she is placed with you, it may be helpful to arrange a visit to your health visitor or child development clinic for assistance. Some children may have learning difficulties resulting from developmental delay. Some of these may not be noticed until the child reaches school age.

What emotional and/or mental health problems might we have to deal with?

Helpful resources

Children Exposed to Parental Substance Misuse: Implications for family placement, edited by Rena Phillips, 2004. A very informative anthology which looks at the effects of tobacco, drugs and alcohol on the foetus, the newborn and the infant, and the implications for family placement. Available from BAAF (Appendix 1).

Problems the child may be born with Neglected or abused children may have different types of mental health difficulties which are not a direct result of neglect or abuse; for example, congenital conditions such as heart disease. If such illnesses are already diagnosed in the child (or if there is an inherited problem that exists in members of the birth family but currently not in the child), you should be fully informed and given advice by social workers and medical advisers. In rare cases, adopted children can develop congenital conditions some time after their adoption. In such situations adoptive parents are advised to contact their adoption agency in the interests of members of their child's birth family.

The developing foetus can also be damaged before birth if the mother was a heavy smoker or drinker, took harmful drugs or neglected herself and her diet.

Problems resulting from abuse or neglect Children needing adoption may experience a range of mental health problems that are a direct result of abuse and/or neglect. These difficulties can be emotional and/or behavioural, and may include: poor self-image and self-esteem; overly aggressive and/or attention-seeking behaviour; inability to form genuine attachment relationships with other adults and/or children; anxious or "vigilant" behaviour; indiscriminate physical contact with strangers; inability to concentrate; lack of sense of "personal space"; and self-injuring or self-stimulating behaviours (e.g. masturbation).

Attachment difficulties This is one of the main problems for children who have experienced abuse, neglect, and the trauma of separation. Attachment, briefly described, is the process of emotional bonding that occurs between infants and their main caregiver (usually mothers) during the first several years of life. During this period the infant learns many aspects of emotions and socialisation from his or her caregiver and forms a secure, loving relationship with that person.

Terms you may need to know

Attention Deficit Hyperactivity Disorder (ADHD) is an impairment of activity and attention control. The diagnostic features are inattention, over-activity (especially in situations requiring calm), and impulsiveness.

Children who have been neglected or abused often display anxious and hyperactive behaviour as a result of insecure emotional attachment. This behaviour may sometimes be interpreted as ADHD or ADD (Attention Deficit Disorder). There is a great deal of controversy about these conditions and whether children diagnosed with ADHD or ADD actually have attachment difficulties rather than ADHD/ADD. It is important to be aware of these issues if you need to consult health professionals about your child's behaviour (see Appendix 2 for ADD organisations).

Attachment: the good news and the difficult news ...

This guide provides only a brief description of attachment difficulties in children. The good news is that there is a growing body of literature and support to help parents and children. Current research shows, for example, that the physical development of the brain can occur throughout life, once the child receives the appropriate stimulation and attachment to a main caregiver.

The difficult news is that children don't overcome attachment difficulties overnight. It takes a lot of perseverance, patience and determination from parents to help children overcome such problems.

So what happens in infants and children who do not have this connection with a main caregiver? Research now indicates that lack of physical contact, stimulation and communication with a main caregiver can inhibit the child from developing social behaviours (such as sharing, learning right and wrong, etc.) which he or she would have learned from the caregiver. It is now known that this lack of contact also affects the growth and development of certain areas of the brain. This then leads to a lack of emotional development (such as knowing how to express emotions verbally, e.g. 'I feel sad'). Children who have not formed an attachment to a main caregiver(s) are described by health professionals as suffering from "attachment difficulties" (also described in professional diagnostic manuals as *Reactive Attachment Disorder*).

Post-traumatic Stress Disorder (PTSD) is a condition that may affect children and adults who have experienced extreme physical or psychological trauma. Thus, children who have suffered intense abuse or neglect or, in some cases, sudden removal from a loved carer or familiar environment, may have difficulties with PTSD.

People who have PTSD suffer recurrent memories of the traumatic stress, rather than being able to "integrate" the traumatic experience into the normal cycle of emotional recovery. When the flashes of traumatic memory occur, the body experiences the same physical and psychological stress as if the event were actually occurring. This leads to physical and behavioural reactions, such as increased heart rate and breathing, sweating, panic, nightmares, eating disorders, aggression and hyperactivity. When a child's body and mind are continually bombarded by such stress, it affects the child's ability to recover a healthy emotional state. The child's behavioural responses to the stress affect his or her ability to socialise, to learn (thus to attend school) and to participate in family life and other "normal" childhood activities. Children who suffer from PTSD should receive professional medical and psychological help.

Helpful resources

Leaflets, booklets, guides

Adoption, Attachment and Development: Making the connection – an outline for adoptive parents, by Caroline Archer, 2001. This 7-page leaflet is available free from Adoption UK. It lists many books that deal with attachment issues in children.

Effects of Early Trauma by Caroline Archer, 1999. A 10-page booklet, available from Adoption UK.

Making Sense of Attachment in Adoptive and Foster Families: An information pack, Adoption UK, 2000. A 96-page guide available from Adoption UK.

Attachment, Trauma and Resilience: Therapeutic caring for children, by Kate Cairns, 2002. Offers a vivid picture of family life with children who have experienced attachment difficulties, loss, abuse and trauma and how the family responded.

See also Section 5 and Appendix 1 and 2 for a detailed list of books, resources, and contact details for the publishers listed here.

It's a piece of cake? Parenting hurt children

This 8-part course devised by Adoption UK is available to adoptive and foster parents through local authorities. The programme is designed to help parents develop understanding and expertise in dealing with attachment issues and the effects of early trauma in children. Parents explore their own expectations and share new and creative parenting strategies. For more information, see Section 5.

Helpful resources

Meeting your child's physical, developmental, emotional and/or behavioural needs

In addition to the post-adoption support services described in Section 5, the following resources may provide information and assistance.

The Anna Freud Centre
A registered charity that provides services to families and children with emotional, behavioural, and developmental difficulties. The Centre also conducts research into the effectiveness of psychotherapy techniques and children's emotional development, including attachment. Treatment is provided to families based on need, not on ability to pay.
21 Maresfield Gardens
London NW3 5SD
Tel: 020 7794 2313
www.annafreudcentre.org

Association for Child Psychology and Psychiatry
An association for professionals of various disciplines who are involved with children. It arranges seminars and publishes professional journals. It does not provide an advice service.
39 – 41 Union Street
London SE1 1SD
Tel: 020 7403 7458
www.acpp.org.uk

Association of Child Psychotherapists (ACP)
A professional organisation for child psychotherapists in the UK. Recognised by the Department of Health as the body which accredits UK training in child and adolescent psychotherapy.
120 West Heath Road
London NW3 7TU
Tel: 020 8458 1609
email: inquiries@acp.uk.net
www.acp.uk.net

British Association for Counselling and Psychotherapy (BACP)
Send a self-addressed, stamped envelope for details of local counsellors and psychotherapists.
BACP House
35 – 37 Albert Street
Rugby
Warwickshire CV21 2SG
Tel: 0870 443 5252 (information)
Monday – Friday 9.30am – 3.00pm
email: bacp@bacp.co.uk
www.bacp.co.uk

The British Association of Psychotherapists (BAP)
The training institution and professional association of psychoanalytic psychotherapists, analytical psychologists (Jungian) and child psychotherapists.

37 Mapesbury Road
London NW2 4HJ
Tel: 020 8452 9823
www.bap-psychotherapy.org

Caspari Foundation (formerly Forum for the Educational Therapy and Therapeutic Teaching, FAETT)

Established in 2000, this organisation promotes educational therapy and therapeutic learning to help children who have emotional barriers that can impair learning. Provides courses for teachers, as well as consultations for children and their parents.

Caspari House, 1 Noel Road
London N1 8HQ
Tel: 020 7704 1977
www.caspari.org.uk

The Centre for Child Mental Health

The aim of the centre is to expand awareness of emotional well-being and mental health of children. It conducts research in child mental health, provides information for parents, teachers, professionals and public, and provides seminars by mental health professionals, covering a range of child mental health topics, including issues that affect adopted children.

2 – 18 Britannia Row, Islington
London N1 8PA
Tel: 020 7354 2913
email: info@childmentalhealth.centre.org
www.childmentalhealthcentre.org

Child Psychotherapy Trust

Provides information about children's emotional development and behaviour; promotes understanding of child psychotherapy and access to child psychotherapy services; and supports training of child psychotherapists.

Star House, 104 – 108 Grafton Road
London NW5 4BD
Tel: 020 7284 1355
Helpline: 020 7485 5510
www.childpsychotherapytrust.org.uk

DDAT (UK) Ltd (formerly Dyslexia, Dyspraxia and Attention Treatment Centre)

Provides assessment, consultation and treatment for children, adolescents and adults who may have dyslexia, dyspraxia or attention difficulties.

Camden House, Warwick Road

Kenilworth
Warwickshire CV8 1TH
Tel: 0870 880 6060/0870 737 0017
email: info@ddat.co.uk
www.ddat.co.uk

Institute of Child Health

Works in partnership with the Great Ormond Street Hospital to form the largest paediatric training and research centre in the UK. The hospital offers the widest range of paediatric specialists in the country.

30 Guildford Street
London WC1N 1EH
Tel: 020 7242 9789
www.ich.ucl.ac.uk

Mentality

The national charity dedicated to the promotion of mental health. Provides a range of services and resources, policy work, campaigning, and practical work. Has experience working with children who are looked after.

134 – 138 Borough High Street
London SE1 1LB
Tel: 020 7716 6777
email: enquiries@mentality.org.uk
www.mentality.org.uk

YoungMinds

A children's mental health charity committed to improving the mental health of all children and young people. Provides information and services, as well as advocacy work within government and professional organisations; conducts training and seminars for professionals; and conducts consultancy work to develop services for children. Also provides **YoungMinds Parents' Information Service** (see Section 5) and **written information** for young people, parents and professionals, such as: Leaflets – *How can psychologists help children?*, *How can child psychotherapists help?*, *How can family therapy help my family?*, *Children and young people get depressed too;* Resources sheets – *ADHD, Education, Depression, Anxiety; YoungMinds* magazine.

102 – 108 Clerkenwell Road
London EC1M 5SA
Tel: 020 7336 8445
email: info@young.minds.org.uk
www.youngminds.org.uk

Taking action ...

... to look after the emotional health of children in foster care and in residential care

In 1996, the National Children's Bureau undertook a 3-year project to identify the mental health needs of children in foster or residential care. The study found that carers are concerned about the mental health of the children in their care and that there is a lack of mental health support for carers from local health authorities. As a result of recent studies in Glasgow, researchers have concluded that, 'A better understanding of the emotional and behavioural difficulties experienced by many looked after children is crucial if appropriate interventions are to be provided. The first step towards this is for every child entering care to have a comprehensive psychological assessment so their individual needs can be identified and met.' [3]

The Government's Quality Protects initiative has set specific targets to improve the mental health of children and local authorities have been given guidance to improve these services.

Won't there be extra "emotional hurdles" for my adopted child as he or she grows up?

Yes. In addition to the possible problems with self-esteem and attachment mentioned earlier, children may have questions about their life history and about their birth family, to varying degrees. The way in which these issues affect your child may be influenced by the child's age at adoption and by the amount of contact he or she has with the birth family. Very young children usually happily accept the story of their adoption, but as they grow old enough to understand the concept of rejection, some children become anxious or withdrawn when adoption is mentioned. Extra sensitivity is required if this seems to be happening. Help is available with this kind of difficulty, so do not hesitate to seek it if you feel uncertain about how to handle it. These issues can affect a child's behaviour without you – or your child – realising it.

It is important to talk openly with your child about his or her life history, and to provide the facts, little by little, as your child becomes old enough to understand them. Many adoptive parents help their children talk about their life history, using the life story book provided by their social worker (see Section 1) and through Child Appreciation Days.[4] Talking about these events openly and in a positive manner will help your child understand his or her life history and come to terms with any difficult issues. There are many resources and organisations that can help both you and your child along the way.

Can I ask the local authority for help after I have adopted my child?

Yes. Many local authorities are trying to keep in touch with adopters, as all voluntary adoption agencies do, by offering a regular newsletter, workshops, social events, etc. However, even if you are not in contact with a local authority, you can ask for help. If it is more than three years since your child was placed, or more than a year since the Adoption Order (whichever is longer), you should approach the local authority

---

3 H. Minnis and C. Del Priori, 'Mental health services for looked after children: implications from two studies', *Adoption & Fostering*, 25: 4, pp 27 – 38.

4 A Child Appreciation Day is used to introduce adopters to those who have significant personal knowledge of the child (e.g. the nursery nurse, the health visitor); these people often have important information and recollections to share with adopters.

Taking action ...

... Understanding current initiatives to co-ordinate health and social services

The Government is developing policies designed to integrate health and social services more closely. For adoptive parents this integration could be immensely beneficial in helping to sort through and co-ordinate services for the physical and emotional difficulties your child might have.

The integrated services would be called "Care Trusts". As yet, policies have not been fully developed nor agreed by the Government. For more information about the development of this policy and how it could affect you, order a free copy of the report, *Care Trusts: Emerging framework* (ref. 23486) from:
Department of Health Publications
PO Box 777, London SE1 6XH

where you live. Otherwise, you should contact the local authority which placed your child with you. The Adoption Support Services Regulations 2003 require the local authority to assess your needs and that of your child for adoption support.

All local authorities in England are required to have a range of adoption support services in their area. These are:

- financial support

- support groups for adoptive parents and adopted children

- support for contact arrangements between adopted children and their birth relatives or other important people

- therapeutic services

- training, respite care and other services to help support the placement

- counselling, advice and information.

You and your child have a right to have an assessment of your needs for adoption support, either those listed above or any others, e.g. help in liaising with schools, help in talking with the child about adoption, etc. The local authority must prepare a written adoption support plan which sets out what it has assessed your support needs are and how it proposes to meet these. Guidance to the regulations states that local authorities must act reasonably in deciding whether to provide adoption support services following an assessment. However, it may not be possible to provide a service to meet every need.

Is it more difficult to adopt a child who has a physical, mental or learning disability?

No. The process for adopting a child with a disability is the same as for any other child. Again, the main concern of the adoption agency will be that you are able to meet the specific needs of that child. Because a disabled child may place different and/or additional pressures on adoptive parents, there are many disabled children waiting for adoption. Many local authorities have recognised this problem and are trying to recruit adoptive parents for these children.

75

The Government's Quality Protects initiative

requires that local authorities 'ensure that children with specific social needs arising out of disability or a health condition are living in families or other appropriate settings in the community where their assessed needs are adequately met and reviewed'.

The Council for Disabled Children has produced a report, *Second Analysis of the Quality Protects Management Action Plans: Services for disabled children and their families*, that details how the objectives from the Quality Protects initiative have addressed the needs of disabled children and their families. It has identified several barriers to taking these forwards including local government reorganisation; difficulties of recruitment of foster carers and adopters; and the difficulty of responding to a constant flow of new legislation and initiatives from central government. There was a general concern that disabled children and young people waited disproportionately longer for placement than non-disabled children.

The Department of Health made available an extra £60 million for disabled children over the three years to March 2004 with a commitment to improving and developing services for disabled children.

Helpful resources

What is a Disability?, by Hedi Argent, 2004.
A guide for children which describes different disabilities and explains what they mean. Available from BAAF (Appendix 1).

Under the NHS and Community Care Act 1990 and the Children Act 1989, social services have a duty to assess the needs of a child with a disability. If you adopt a disabled child, you have the right to ask for your child's needs to be assessed by the social services department and you also have the right to ask for an assessment for yourself – this will be under the new Carers and Disabled Children Act. Once your child's needs have been assessed, the social worker will agree with you what services are to be provided.

These services could include practical assistance in the home; provision of recreational or educational facilities; home adaptations; travel, meals, and other assistance; a telephone and ancillary equipment. Other services may be provided under the Children Act but these may be discretionary. You will need to find out what is available from your local authority and you can contact the Contact a Family helpline for more information.

Will we be more likely to receive financial support if we adopt a disabled child?

According to the Adoption Support Services Regulations 2003, an allowance may be paid if the child 'needs special care which requires a greater expenditure of resources by reason of illness, disability, emotional or behavioural difficulties or the continuing consequences of past abuse or neglect'. You will be "assessed" for any allowance for which you may be eligible. For more information about financial support, see Section 2 of this handbook.

Families of disabled children may also be entitled to additional support, such as mobility allowance or attendance allowance. For more information about these allowances, contact your local Benefits Agency.

Helpful resources

If your child has a physical or mental difficulty

There are many organisations which support children with specific difficulties. Those listed here are "umbrella" organisations that provide general support regarding adoption and/or physical or mental difficulties.

Contact a Family
Provides information for parents on over 2,000 rare medical conditions, including information about support groups, and publishes a useful directory, *The CAF Directory of Specific Conditions and Rare Disorders 2002*. There is also a freephone helpline for parents seeking information regarding help for disabled children.
209 – 211 City Road, London EC1V 1JN
Helpline: 0808 808 3555 Monday – Friday, 10am – 4pm
Tel: 020 7608 8700
Minicom: 020 7608 8702
email: jim@cafamily.org.uk
www.cafamily.org.uk

Council for Disabled Children
Promotes collaborative work between different organisations providing services and support for children and young people with disabilities and special educational needs. Offers a range of services, including consultancy, training, information, publications and conferences.
8 Wakley Street, London EC1
Tel: 020 7843 1900
email: cdc@ncb.org.uk
www.ncb.org.uk/cdc/index

Publications

The Placement of Children with Disabilities
BAAF, 1998.
This Practice Note, mainly aimed at social workers, also contains very useful information for carers and parents about family placement of children with severe to profound disabilities.

Whatever happened to Adam? Stories of disabled people who were adopted or fostered
by Hedi Argent, BAAF, 1998.
This remarkable book tells the stories of 20 young disabled people and the families who chose to care for them. The book follows the children's life journeys from joining their new families, through childhood and adolescence and into preparation for adulthood. A powerful and timely reminder that adoption and fostering can be tremendously rewarding for disabled children and for their adoptive and foster families.

When your Child has Special Needs: A guide for parents who care for a child with a disability, special need or rare disorder
Contact a Family, 2002.
An extremely useful guide that gives pointers to the kind of help that is available when caring for a child with a disability, special need or disorder.

Taking action ...

... to improve mental health services for children and adolescents

Child and Adolescent Mental Health Services: Everybody's Business

Produced by the National Assembly for Wales, outlines the 10-year programme to improve the range and quality of child and mental health services in Wales. Copies of the report are available from the Primary and Community Healthcare Division,
Tel: 02920 823 480 or from www.wales.gov.uk

Child and Adolescent Mental Health Services Innovation Projects

are being initiated throughout the United Kingdom to offer direct mental health services to children, as well as consultation, support and training for teachers, health visitors and social workers. Among the 24 projects currently underway are:

● **Scallywags** – a community-based programme in Cornwall to provide early intervention for young children with behavioural and emotional difficulties. More information available from www.cornwall.gov.uk/scallywags email: scallywags@cornwall.gov.uk

● **Support Service for Looked After Children** in Sheffield offers a range of therapeutic work for children in foster care, residential units, with birth families, and some children after adoption.
www.nspcc.org.uk

● **Child Behaviour Intervention Initiative** in Leicestershire and Rutland – an early intervention partnership among health, education and social care providers to intervene at an early stage with children who have emotional and behavioural problems.
Tel: 0116 225 2888
www.lc.ac.uk/greenwood/child_behaviour_intervention.htm

Framework for the Assessment of Children in Need and their Families

These are guidelines, produced by the Department of Health, to help social services professionals assess looked after children and children moving to adoption. For more information contact the Department for Education and Skills or access www.dfes.gov.uk

The National Clinical Director for Children

has recently been appointed to oversee development of the Children's National Service Framework. This initiative is intended to co-ordinate all NHS plans for children's services. Child and adolescent mental health and emotional well-being is one of six key areas to be addressed by the framework. For more information, see www.dh.gov.uk

The National Institute for Mental Health in England (NIMHE)

is being created to help staff in health and social care implement policy to improve outcomes for people using mental health services. For more information, contact the Department of Health or access www.nimhe.org.uk.

... to ensure your child receives the care to which he or she is entitled

Current legislation regarding children in England and Wales promotes the provision of *co-ordinated*, quality health services for children. This legislation may support your case if you think your child is not receiving needed services. Copies of the legislation are available on www.dh.gov.uk/PolicyAndGuidance/HealthAndSocialCare Topics/ChildrenServices/fs/en

Children's Services Plans

These are broad strategic plans designed to co-ordinate all services for vulnerable children, such as Education Development Plans, Early Years Development Plans, and Behaviour Support Plans. Co-ordination of all plans required for vulnerable children will be provided by local councils, with the full participation of NHS organisations (required by the "duty of partnership" described in the Health Act 1999).

Health Quality Service (HQS)

Runs accreditation schemes for hospitals and community health services, and is developing a quality accreditation scheme for child and adolescent mental health services. Standards cover issues of access, efficiency, effectiveness, service user's experience and staff experience.
15 Whitehall
London SW1A 2DD
www.hqs.org.uk

Helpful resources

Organisations and information to help adopted children and adults who were adopted as children

Adoption in My Life A videotape and audiotape programme developed as part of a project funded by the Department of Health to determine the needs of young people (mid-teens – early 20s) who were adopted as children. The programmes follow the young people as they describe their experiences, childhood to present, and some who search for answers to their identity.
Available from:
Catholic Children's Society (Nottingham)
7 Colwick Road
Nottingham NG2 5FR
Tel: 0115 955 8811
email: enquiries@ccsnotts.co.uk
www.ccsnotts.co.uk

NORCAP – supporting adults affected by adoption
A self-help support group for all parties to adoption. It offers advice for members on searching and a research service. It can play an intermediary role for those seeking renewed contact. NORCAP maintains a successful Contact Register and publishes a newsletter three times a year.
NORCAP
112 Church Road, Wheatley
Oxon OX33 1LU
Tel: 01865 875 000
email: enquiries@norcap.org.uk
www.norcap.org.uk

Talk Adoption
A free, confidential national helpline for young people, up to 25 years old, who have a link with adoption, whether adoptee, friend or relative.
Tuesday – Friday 3 – 9pm
Tel: 0808 808 1234
www.talkadoption.org.uk

Who Cares? Trust
A registered charity that promotes services for children and young people in public care, those who have left public care, and those whose lives continue to be affected by their care experiences. The Trust ensures the opinions of those directly affected by care are heard in the planning and provision of services for them. Publishes the *Who Cares?* magazine.
Kemp House, 152 – 160 City Road
London EC1V 2NP
Tel: 020 7251 3117
email: mailbox@thewhocarestrust.org.uk
www.thewhocarestrust.org.uk

To contact birth parents/relatives

The Adoption Contact Register
for England & Wales
Office of National Statistics
The General Register Office
Adoptions Section
Smedley Hydro
Trafalgar Road
Southport
Merseyside PR8 2HH
Tel: 0151 471 4831
email: admin@adoptionregister.net
www.adoptionregister.net

for Scotland
Birthlink
c/o Family Care
21 Castle Street
Edinburgh EH2 3DN
Tel: 0131 225 6441

General and health resources for children and young adults

Connexions
A service that provides advice and support for young people (aged 13–19) in England, with priority given to young people who are '… at greatest risk of not making a successful transition to adulthood'. A network of Connexions advisors helps young people with decisions about life, education and careers. Forty-seven local partnerships, which you can contact, are listed on their website: www.connexions.gov.uk

Depression Alliance
Promotes greater understanding of depression to reduce the stigma associated with it. Produces booklet, *The Young Person's Guide to Stress*.
35 Westminster Bridge Road
London SE1 7JB
Tel: 0845 123 2320
www.depressionalliance.org

LifeBytes
A health website for young people (aged 11–14) that provides health education, but not health advice. Produced by the Department of Health and the Health Education Authority.
www.lifebytes.gov.uk

Scottish Health on the Web (SHOW)
Provided by the NHS in Scotland, this site provides general health information, contact details of all NHS Trusts, and links to other websites.
www.show.scot.nhs.uk

UK Health Centre

A general internet health resources library. Provides links to literature and other resources.

www.healthcentre.org.uk

UK Youth (formerly Youth Clubs UK)

A network of local providers of youth services. Delivers and supports voluntary work and informal education for young people. Produces many publications for young people and youth workers about emotional/behavioural issues.

2nd Floor, Kirby House
20 – 24 Kirby Street
London EC1N 8TS
Tel: 020 7242 4045
email: info@ukyouth.org
www.ukyouth.org

Carers and Disabled Children Act 2000

Implemented on 1 April 2001, this is a government initiative launched in 1988 which requires local authorities to ensure that children with specific social needs arising out of disability or a health condition are living in families or other appropriate settings in the community where their assessed needs are adequately met and reviewed. This Act gives local councils the power to provide certain services directly to carers following assessment, even where the person cared for has refused an assessment. People with parental responsibility for a child also have the right to an assessment.

Local councils also have the power to make direct payments to:

- carers to meet their own assessed needs (this includes 16 and 17-year-old carers);
- 16 and 17-year-old disabled young people;
- parents of a disabled child, to purchase services to meet the assessed needs of the disabled child and family.

Parents or young people may want a direct payment because they think that existing services do not meet their child's, or their own needs, and they believe that they can make better arrangements themselves.

Assessments are made with reference to both the Children Act 1989, and the Department of Health Framework for the Assessment of Children in Need and their Families (2000).

5

for adoptive parents

In this section

- identify and focus on your own particular needs as adoptive parents

- consider some of the most common emotions adoptive parents encounter and why these feelings occur

- find the resources, organisations and services that can help you help yourself through the various emotions of the adoption experience

5 for adoptive parents

B Y ITS VERY NATURE, adoption is a process that has its ups and its downs. The first four sections of this book describe many of the procedural, financial and emotional pitfalls that can potentially turn a happy experience into a stressful and frustrating nightmare.

The experience of having a child, by birth or by adoption, is always a journey into the unknown – none of us knows if our expected child will have any physical or emotional difficulties. Yet, because adoption is a *process* of bringing a child into your home and family, you can be fairly certain you will encounter some degree of difficulty at some point along the way.

Acceptance is the first step to a "smooth" adoption

The first step in making the experience of adoption as smooth as possible is to accept that adopting a child is different from giving birth to a child. You will have to adjust your preconceptions and your expectations about parenthood and having children. We hope the resources and information provided in this guide will help you cope with the procedural and physical difficulties you might encounter. The emotional difficulties involved in adoption are a different battle altogether – these are the experiences that challenge you and change you. These are the experiences we discuss in this section.

Adoptive parents' needs are important too

Adoption focuses on meeting the needs of a child. But this does not mean we should ignore the needs of adoptive parents. After all, if you do not look after your own physical and emotional needs, you won't be able to provide much help to your child.

Yet, every adoption is an individual event and everyone responds differently to it. So, while we can't predict every emotional response you'll have throughout your adoption – and thus offer "answers" to every difficulty – we can describe some *general* feelings that most adopters experience and offer some *general* advice. Although it is difficult to "avoid" having certain experiences and feelings throughout adoption, just being *aware* of the feelings you might have can often help you get through particular experiences more easily.

Let's take a minute to discuss some of the "lows" of the adoptive parent's emotional rollercoaster. Why would this be helpful? If you have not yet adopted, or only recently adopted, it can help you prepare to expect some of these "lows" and, hopefully, to be less surprised if you experience these emotions. If you have already adopted, perhaps reading about some of the most common emotions adoptive parents face as a result of common experiences of the adoption process will reassure you that other adopters have similar feelings. This can help bolster your confidence as an adoptive parent.

Taking action ...

... to assess risk and resilience in prospective carers

Research is currently underway to develop effective tools that will enable social workers and others to assess the emotional and psychological resilience of prospective adoptive parents or foster carers. The intent of this research is not to further scrutinise carers, but to ensure that, as adoptive/foster parents, you are matched with a child whose emotional, psychological and/or physical demands will not exceed your abilities to meet such demands. Current studies include:

Assessment of Carers by A. Bifulco and G. Thomas
This study is being conducted by Parents for Children, in conjunction with the Lifespan Research Group at the University of London. Researchers are examining the benefits of using research-based, standardised interview assessment tools when assessing carers. Specific topics of this research include making assessments faster, matching children and prospective parents more accurately, and assessing families' needs for post-placement support.

The Use of the Adult Attachment Interview: Implications for assessment in adoption and foster care by M. Steele, J. Kaniuk, J. Hodges, C. Haworth and S. Huss
This research is being conducted at the Anna Freud Centre in London. Researchers have studied the use of the Adult Attachment Interview (AAI) in assessing attachment in a group of parents who voluntarily adopted children with developmental delays. The AAI is commonly used in researching parent–child relationships, but has not previously been used in the assessment of carers. Contact the centre at www.annafreudcentre.org for more information (see Appendix 2).

Feelings and emotions adoptive parents commonly encounter throughout the adoption experience

"Instant" parenthood Despite the months (perhaps years) of planning for your adopted child, it is difficult to be fully prepared for the child's arrival in your home. You can easily prepare for your child's physical needs. But being ready for your and your child's emotional responses (no matter what age child you have adopted) is altogether different. This is particularly true for individuals or couples who have not parented a child before – either born to them, fostered or adopted. The first few months after the placement can be a time of joy, but may also bring feelings of guilt, depression, perhaps even panic. The question, 'Have we done the right thing?', might enter your head more than a few times after the child is first placed with you or after the adoption goes through.

Helpful resources

Parents Are Linked (PAL)

This service, co-ordinated by Adoption UK, links people who have particular questions about adoption with people who can provide useful information based upon their own experiences.

The service is available to Adoption UK members. As a member, you can phone Adoption UK, register your question(s) with the PAL database, and then be matched with someone who may be able to help you. For more information, contact Adoption UK (see Appendix 2).

It is important, at this stage, to remember you are a new parent or new to parenting this child and have taken on an immense challenge. You may find it helpful to share your true feelings with others – especially with other adoptive parents. It will also be important to give yourself "respite" time away from your child in order to "rest and recoup" from the stresses of parenting an adopted child.

"Sharing" your child When your child is finally placed with you, it is common to want to immerse the child in your family life – in a sense, to make the child "your own". It can be difficult, at this time, to continually remind yourself that your child is the focus of the adoption process and that you might have to endure some experiences (such as visits with foster carers and/or birth parents) that you may not enjoy, but which may be in the best interests of your child. It can be painful, for example, to see your newly adopted child run to his or her former foster carers' arms for comfort, or to feel your child reject you in favour of other people he or she has known previously. Moreover, children who have attachment difficulties (see Section 4) are experts at manipulating other adults to their own advantage, while rejecting you in the process. When your child is first placed with you, you may feel surprised, confused and frustrated by such experiences.

"Attachment? What attachment?" There will be times when you may have to face the issue of "love" for your child. Do you "love" him or her? Or do you feel sympathy, empathy, even "caring" and responsibility, rather than unconditional love? You will not be the first adoptive parent to ask yourself these questions. These feelings arise because many children who have been neglected or abused do not exhibit any vulnerability – that is, they do not show any signs that they really "need" parents. So, you may find it hard to love a child who seemingly doesn't "need" you.

Helpful resources

Books about attachment difficulties and parenting children who have attachment difficulties (see also Section 4)

- *Attachment Theory, Child Maltreatment and Family Support: A practice and assessment model* by David Howe *et al*, Macmillan, 1999.

- *Attachment, Trauma and Resilience: Therapeutic caring for children* by Kate Cairns, BAAF, 2002.

- *Facilitating Developmental Attachment: The road to emotional recovery and behavioural change in foster and adopted children* by Daniel A. Hughes, Jason Aronson, Inc., 1997.

- *First Steps in Parenting the Child Who Hurts: Tiddlers & Toddlers* by Caroline Archer, Jessica Kingsley Publishers, 1999.

- *Fostering Attachments: Long-term outcomes in family group care* by Brian Cairns, BAAF, 2004.

- *Making Sense of Attachment in Adoptive and Foster Families: An information pack*. Available from Adoption UK

- *Next Steps in Parenting the Child Who Hurts: Tykes & Teens* by Caroline Archer, Jessica Kingsley Publishers,1999.

A list of books of interest to families living with, and professionals working with, children with attachment and behavioural difficulties is available from Adoption UK (see Appendix 2).

In addition, children with attachment difficulties may have behaviours that make you feel rejected. These are the times when your commitment as an adoptive parent overrides all other emotions – you stick with it because you believe in what you are doing, you believe in your child, and you believe in your child's capacity to overcome his or her difficulties.

During these times, it is important to seek support from others – social workers, counsellors, mental health professionals, post-adoption support organisations, and other adoptive parents. It is also imperative to acknowledge your own feelings about being an adoptive parent and to remember that, as adoptive parents, we may not have begun our relationship with our children with immediate "love". We may have felt sympathy and care for the child, initially, but in some cases, true love – the ability to love the child when the child pushes rejection right at you – may take years to develop.

Remember, also, that many adoptive parents don't have the benefit of a gestation period or a "bonding time" with a young infant. Parents of children adopted after the age of 2½–3 years are presented with a walking, talking individual with his or her own personality, and with the complex effects of early neglect and/or trauma. Consequently, it will take time for you to develop a deep bond with your child, just as your child will take time to attach to you.

Helpful resources

Training and information for parents

Finding a Way Through: Therapeutic caring for children, Kate Cairns in conversation with John Simmonds. A powerful video-taped discussion which offers foster carers and adoptive parents ways of reaching out to damaged children. Available for £35.25 from BAAF (see Appendix 2).

Adoption and Attachment – A one-year, part-time training course for social workers, therapists, foster carers and adoptive parents. For more information contact Family Futures (see Appendix 2).

***It's a Piece of Cake?* A parent support programme developed by adopters for adopters** Provided by Adoption UK through local authorities. This eight-module course is designed specifically to help adoptive parents gain insight into their children and to help them in their challenging role with their children. Contact Adoption UK for more information (see Appendix 2).

The Impact of Trauma on Children and How Foster Families and Adoptive Families Can Help Them A videotape presentation by Dan Hughes, PhD, a psychologist who specialises in helping foster and adopted children. Dr Hughes discusses how parents can help children develop positive attachments and presents strategies for coping with oppositional behaviour. Available for £100 from Family Futures (see Appendix 2).

YoungMinds Supporting Parents campaign Provides information packs for parents and carers. The packs provide information about promoting your child's mental health, recognising when there may be a problem, and how to find help for mental health problems. A separate pack is available for GPs and other health professionals. Both packs are available free from YoungMinds (see Appendix 2).

'Let me explain about adoption ...' A while after having a child placed, many parents develop an understanding of their child and learn how to respond to their child's various behaviours. However, problems often arise when trying to help the "outside" world understand their children and their children's needs. Daily life may then become a series of stressful events, when activities, such as dealing with schools, grandparents, even those after-school swimming lessons, become difficult because the people involved don't understand your child's behaviours. You may hesitate to discuss adoption with these people, because you don't want to appear to make "excuses" for your child's behaviour. Often, however, open communication is the best policy. The general public usually is unaware of the effects of early trauma on children. Explaining these effects and "educating" others in how best to respond to your child will not only help your child now, but will also help others respond more positively to your child in the future.

A question of guilt and anger Parenting a child who has attachment difficulties is tough. At times, your anger and frustration with the child may exceed levels you never thought existed within you. You may then begin to question your abilities as a parent, feel guilty about your own anger and reactions to your child, and may feel inadequate to the task of parenting an adopted child. These feelings can be reinforced when other well-meaning people around us (grandparents, friends, social workers, spouses) do not see or understand the child's behaviours. 'Why are you so "uptight"?', they wonder. 'Why are you so strict with your child?' They don't understand your emotions, because they don't spend the same amount of time with the child as you do and they don't see that your child may have rejecting behaviours that are targeted at you – the main caregiver. These will be times of extreme frustration and anxiety for you. It will be important for you to seek the support of the post-adoption organisations and services available to you.

Looking to the future, but acknowledging the past The fact that your child is adopted and that he or she has had experiences not shared with you, is something you can never change. Often, adoptive parents may feel reluctant to talk with their child about the past. You may even feel uncomfortable being open about your child's adoption with those around you. Especially in the first few months after the child is placed with you, it is tempting to try to forget the child's past entirely in order to focus on your future with your child.

Taking action ...

... government guidance about post-adoption support

The National Adoption Standards for England, published by the Department of Health in August 2001, provide the following guidance regarding post-adoption support. It is important to keep in mind that the purpose of the National Standards is to improve the quality of adoption services by outlining goals adoption services are expected to achieve. Local authorities are expected to meet the standards from April 2003.

Guidance to local councils: 'There will be clear policies for adoption, including post-adoption services, which are set out in Children and Young People's Strategic Plans or equivalent local plans.' (Section E, Councils, No. 2)

'Councils, with the relevant agencies ... will provide or commission a comprehensive range of pre- and post-adoption services consistent with any national framework or regulation. These will facilitate and support adoption and meet the needs of children who move between local authority areas. Criteria for access to services will be clear, concise and understandable.' (Section E, Councils, No. 6)

Guidance for adoptive parents: 'There will be access to a range of multi-agency support services before, during and after adoption. Support services will include practical help, professional advice, financial assistance where needed and information about local and national support groups and services.' (Section C, Adoptive Parents, No. 3)

Helpful resources

General organisations that provide help for parents

Increasingly, local authority and voluntary agencies have post-adoption specialists dedicated to providing services for adoptive families. It is worth checking what is available from the agency from whose care your child was adopted, the agency that prepared you to adopt, the local authority where you now live, and any consortia or specialist agencies. Below are several organisations that can provide such support.

Family Futures Consortium

A service for families who adopt or foster. Provides an assessment service that involves parents and children (and other family members, if necessary). Also provides an intensive attachment programme that focuses on the child and includes parent participation in a non-judgemental manner. Provides seminars and training programmes for parents, carers and social workers to help support families and children. Also provides courses to health authorities, social services departments, solicitors and children's guardians.
35A Britannia Row
Islington
London N1 8QH
Tel: 020 7354 4161
email: contact@familyfutures.co.uk
www.familyfutures.co.uk

Fostering Network (previously National Foster Care Association)

Offers advice and information and also has a series of leaflets available on fostering. Also publishes the magazine *Foster Care*.
87 Blackfriars Road
London SE1 8HA
Tel: 020 7620 6400
www.fostering.net

International Foster Care Organisation (IFCO)

A voluntary organisation based in the Netherlands committed to improving the quality of service given to children and young people in care, and to developing standards for organisations and individual carers. IFCO provides international and regional conferences, a newsletter, website and supports the IFCO Youth in Care Project.
email: denhaagoffice@ifco.info
www.internationalfostering.org

National Family and Parenting Institute

An independent charity set up to enhance the value and quality of family life. Works to support parents in bringing up children, to promote the well-being of families, and to make society more family friendly. Organises an annual Parents' Week, to celebrate families and parents. Provides 'Pals for Parents' service, a parents' befriending programme.
430 Highgate Studios
53 – 79 Highgate Road
London NW5 1TL
Tel: 020 7424 3460
email: info@nfpi.org
www.nfpi.org

Our Place

A registered charity that provides support for families who foster or adopt. The centre offers workshops for parents and for professionals, activities for children, private consultations for parents, a resource room, and opportunities to meet other adoptive/foster parents. It produces a bi-monthly bulletin of upcoming activities and workshops.There is no fee or geographical restriction to attend the centre. Families attending must have at least one adopted or foster child living in the home. The centre is open Monday – Friday 10am – 6pm, with some evening and weekend sessions.
139 Fishponds Road
Eastville
Bristol BS5 6PR
Tel: 0117 951 2433
email: ourplace1@btconnect.com

Parentline Plus

A confidential helpline that provides information and emotional support to parents.
Tel: 0808 800 2222
Textphone: 0800 783 6783
www.parentlineplus.co.uk

Positive Parenting Publications and Programmes

Provides information, resources and training for parents and those who support them.
2A South Street
Gosport
Hampshire PO12 1ES
Tel: 023 9252 8787
www.parenting.org.uk

YoungMinds Parents' Information Service

A telephone service provided by YoungMinds (see Section 4) that gives information and advice for anyone with concerns about the mental health of a child or young person.
Tel: 0800 018 2138
www.youngminds.org.uk/pis

Helpful resources

Talking about Adoption to your Adopted Child

by Marjorie Morrison, BAAF, 2004 (3rd edition). A useful guide that explains how and when to explain to your child that he or she is adopted. Many other books on this topic are available. Contact Adoption UK or BAAF for details (see Appendix 2).

However, in keeping your child's needs at the centre of your thinking, it is important to be aware of signals from your child that he or she needs to talk about and affirm his or her past. The details you choose to discuss with your child and the timing of these discussions depends solely upon your child's age and ability to understand certain concepts. After your child has been with you for some time and your attachment deepens, it will become easier to discuss the past. As you focus on your child's needs, you will soon find the right balance of acknowledging, in a healthy way, the facts of your child's adoption and past history. And, as your child's attachment to you becomes more secure, you will become more comfortable with the issue of contact with birth family members.

In short, it's important to live life "normally", while becoming aware of how your child expresses his or her need to affirm the past. "Drip feed" information to your child, bit by bit – you'll soon become familiar with signs that your child needs to talk about the past.

Give your child small portions of information at opportune moments – often, the casual moments are the most effective – in the car, on the way home from school, for example. It doesn't have to be a long, "prepared" discussion. Just affirming the past in a matter-of-fact way will help your child to incorporate his or her story into life, and a healthy self-image and sense of being.

Helpful resources

Adoption Support Services

There are many well-established post-adoption services that provide a service for adoptive families, adopted people and birth parents whose children were adopted. Many of them offer advice and counselling both in person but also on the telephone or by correspondence. Some of them also organise events.

Your local authority has a duty to offer an adoption support service so you can always contact them to see what is available; many now have an adoption support services worker. If you need specialist support or advice that they cannot provide, they will be able to refer you to a specialist service that will be able to help. Many voluntary agencies also offer a post-adoption service, although, of course, they don't have a statutory duty to do so as do local authorities.

Below we provide a list of independent post-adoption centres.

After Adoption Network A group formed within Adoption UK to help adoptive parents share information and support. You must be a member of Adoption UK to join the network. As a member, you will be given a list of adoptive families in the network who you may contact through meetings or by telephone. For more information, contact Adoption UK (see Appendix 2).

NORCAP (Supporting adults affected by adoption)
112 Church Road
Wheatley
Oxfordshire OX33 1LU
Tel: 01865 875 000
www.norcap.org.uk

ENGLAND

London

After Adoption
85 Moorgate
London EC2M 6SA
Tel: 020 7628 3443
Action line: 0800 056 8578
email: info@afteradoption.org.uk
www.afteradoption.org.uk

Post Adoption Centre
5 Torriano Mews
Torriano Avenue
London NW5 2RZ
Tel: 020 7284 0555
Advice line: 020 7485 2931 Monday, Tuesday, Wednesday, Friday 10am – 1pm, Thurs. 5.30 – 7.30 pm
Action line: 0800 056 8578
www.postadoptioncentre.org.uk

North and Northeast

After Adoption

12–14 Chapel Street
Manchester M3 7NH
Tel 0161 839 4932
email: information@afteradoption.org.uk
www.afteradoption.org.uk

After Adoption Northeast

2nd floor, Aiden House
Tynegate Business Centre, Sunderland Road
Gateshead NE8 3HU
Tel: 0191 478 8396
Action line: 0800 056 8578
email: info@afteradoption.org.uk
www.afteradoption.org.uk

After Adoption Merseyside

60 Duke Street
Liverpool L1 5AA
Action line: 0800 056 8578

North East Post Adoption Service

Royal Quays Community Centre
Prince Consort Way
North Shields
Tyne & Wear NE29 6XB
Tel: 0191 296 6064
Fax: 0191 296 6064
email: nepas@nepas.org
www.nepas.org

Oxfordshire

Parents and Children Together (PACT)

A new regional, multi-agency resource with a three-year
grant to develop services that local authorities may buy
into and to establish specialist consultancy services in post
adoption, that emphasises multi-agency co-ordination.
The PACT On-line Post Adoption Service, currently under
development, will provide a 24-hour information service
via a website, and interactive on-line advice and
counselling services during weekends and evenings.
PACT
FREEPOST (SCE6005)
Reading RG1 4ZR
Tel: 0800 731 1845
email: info@pactcharity.org
www.pactcharity.org

Post-adoption LINK

covering Bedfordshire, Cambridgeshire, Essex,
Hertfordshire, Norfolk, Peterborough, and Suffolk
Barnardo's
54 Head Street
Colchester C01 1PB

Tel: 01206 562 438
email: newfamilies.colchester@barnardos.org.uk

South West Adoption Network (SWAN)

covering Bath, North East Somerset, Bristol,
Gloucestershire, South Gloucestershire, Swindon
Leinster House, Leinster Avenue
Knowle
Bristol BS4 1NL
Tel: 0845 601 2459 Monday – Wednesday 10 – 12,
1:30 – 3:30 pm, Monday evenings 6 – 8 pm
email: admin@swan-adoption.org.uk
www.swan-adoption.org.uk

West Midlands

Adoption Support
(formerly West Midlands Post-adoption Service)

Suite A, 6th Floor
Albany House
Hurst Street
Birmingham B5 4BD
Tel: 0121 666 6014
email: adoptionsupport@tiscali.co.uk
www.adoptionsupport.co.uk

Yorkshire

After Adoption Yorkshire

31 Moor Road
Headingley
Leeds LS6 4BG
Tel: 0113 230 2100
email: info@afteradoptionyorkshire.org.uk
www.afteradoptionyorkshire.org.uk

WALES

After Adoption West Wales

Agricultural House, Ty Amaeth
32 Cambrian Place
Carmarthen SA31 1QG
Tel: 01267 242 968
Helpline: 0800 0568 578
email: camarthen@aadoption.fsbusiness.co.uk
www.afteradoption.org.uk

After Adoption South Wales

2nd Floor, Dominion House North
Dominion Arcade, Queen Street
Cardiff CF10 2AR
Action line: 0800 056 8578

After Adoption Swansea

Swansea YMCA
1 The Kingsway
Swansea SA1 5JQ
Action line: 0800 056 8578

After Adoption Gwent
Torfaen People's Centre
Trosnant House
Trosnant Street
Pontypool
Torfaen NP4 8AT
Action line: 0800 056 8578

After Adoption North Wales
PO Box 52
Oswestry SY10 7ZT
Action line: 0800 056 8578

Birthlink
21 Castle Street, Edinburgh EH2 3DN
Tel: 0131 225 6441
www.birthlink.org.uk

Scottish Adoption Advice Service
16 Sandyford Place, Glasgow G3 7NB
Tel: 0141 339 0772
email: saas@barnardos.org.uk
www.barnardos.org.uk

What can we do if we have trouble handling our child's behaviour?

You can begin by visiting your GP and requesting referral to a consultant child psychologist, psychiatrist or psychotherapist. You could also consult the organisations and services listed in Section 4 as well as those in this section. In addition, local authorities and voluntary adoption agencies provide post-adoption support but services available from different agencies are variable. Contact your agency to find out what they offer.

Will we be able to have adoption support services from a local authority, even if we adopted several years ago?

Yes. This is described in Section 4. Remember that approaching professionals at a post-adoption/adoption support centre, or adoption or adoption support workers in your local authority will be important, especially at times of crises, as these professionals will have a good understanding of adoption and therefore could be particularly helpful.

About disruption

"Disruption" is a term commonly used by social workers to describe an adoption (or foster placement) that does not work out.

A placement can disrupt (i.e. break down) for many reasons: for instance, if the child is unable to bond or attach to the adoptive parents; if the child has difficulties for which the adoptive parents were not adequately prepared; or if there is not adequate adoption support for the family.

Needless to say, disrupted adoptions bring immense grief, guilt and anger for both the adoptive parents and for the child. Some local authorities and adoption agencies provide "disruption meetings" for ongoing support to families who have experienced disruption. According to the National Adoption Standards for England 'where an adoption is at risk of breaking down, all agencies involved in the placement will co-operate to provide support and information to all parties without delay. When an adoption has broken down, all agencies involved will co-operate to provide support to the child and the adoptive parents, and ensure that the birth parents are informed.'[1]

1 *National Adoption Standards for England*, Department of Health, 2001

Helping yourself and helping your child

Hundreds of children in the UK need adoptive families. These children are in need of homes in which they can grow and mature within a loving and secure environment. But adoption certainly is not an "easy" road to travel for these children or for their adoptive parents, and it takes a certain type of parent to make the personal sacrifices required of adopters.

As we stated previously, the purpose of this guide is to help you to help yourself on your journey through adoption. No matter what stage you're at in the process – for example, just considering adoption, waiting to be matched with a child, or seeking post-adoption help many years after your child's placement – there are a rapidly increasing number of services and resources which can help you.

Every week, almost 100 children in Britain are legally adopted. New families are formed. The interplay of personalities and complex issues faced by both the child and the adults creates unique and varied experiences for the adoptive family. You can be certain, therefore, that you may meet other adoptive families whose experiences might be similar to yours, but rarely exactly the same. Because no two adoptions are the same, you also may encounter services (for example, school and health services) which have little experience of the problems you face with your adopted child. Increased publicity and media attention about adoption increases the general public's understanding of these issues. Yet, despite such publicity and the increasing focus on post-adoption services, you are very likely to encounter a significant lack of knowledge and/or understanding about adoption within the general public.

So, what can you do to help yourself?

Firstly, use this guide to communicate with others: with your child's teachers, doctors, babysitter or childminder, birth family members, your own family members, and any other people your child may interact with frequently. Use the guide to inform them about certain issues and/or to find more specific information about these issues.

Secondly, think laterally and creatively! If you and your child are facing specific problems, be aware that solutions to the problem may not always be obvious or straightforward. And remember that there may be several interacting issues that underlie one problem. If, for example, your eight-year-old son still has significant problems with soiling and wetting (even though he has been with you for four years),

Help us to help you!

Because the adoption process and associated services are developing and changing so rapidly, this guide may not provide all the answers you may need. Inevitably, with new government initiatives and rapid growth in post-adoption services, you may come across organisations, publications or services that are not listed here. If so, please inform us.

you may have several "causes" to consider: insecurity, anxiety, physical problems, and attachment issues, to name a few. But, thinking "laterally", you may also have to consider that your son may never have had any formal toilet training, like most toddlers. This is a consideration that, understandably, may never have crossed your mind while you were going through the adoption process four years earlier.

As an adoptive parent, you will be challenged, almost daily, to come up with creative strategies to address your child's needs. Use this guide as a starting point for information, and remember that you may have to tailor some of the information and advice in order to suit your child's particular needs.

Parenting children, in general, is not an easy task. Being an adoptive parent adds its own unique challenges. But, by sharing information in a direct, factual and creative manner, adoptive parents can reduce the stress of unexpected problems, address issues in a calm, practical and informed manner, and look forward to a successful and rewarding experience.

Appendix 1

Books, reports, magazines, leaflets, videos, publishers

The organisations and publications listed in this handbook are for readers' information and reference. The listing of these organisations and publications does not necessarily constitute their endorsement or promotion by BAAF or by the author.

The publications listed here are an alphabetical compilation of most of the publications listed within this Handbook, and are only a sample of the information available.

Books for prospective adopters/adoptive parents

Adopted Children Speaking by Caroline Thomas and Verna Beckford, BAAF, 1999. *Provides moving and poignant testimonies which offer revealing insights into children's feelings about adoption.*

Adopters on Adoption: Reflections on parenthood and children by David Howe, BAAF, 1996. *This absorbing collection of personal stories covers topics including assessment and preparation, feelings towards birth mothers, and biology, infertility, and parenting secure children.*

Adopting a Child by Jenifer Lord, BAAF, 2002. *This guide describes what adoption means and how to go about it, including procedures and practices, legal requirements and the costs involved.*

'Adoption after bereavement' by Eve Hopkirk, *Adoption & Fostering*, 26:1, BAAF, 2002.

Adoption: A guide for court users The Court Service. *See Appendix 2 for contact details.*

Adoption Handbook: A directory of adoption related services, Adoptive Parents Association of Ireland, 1998. *See Appendix 2 for contact details.*

Adoption Now: Law, regulations, guidance and standards by Fergus Smith and Roy Stewart with Deborah Cullen, BAAF, 2003. *A handy spiral-bound pocket book, covering all essential information on the law, regulations, guidance and standards relating to adoption today.*

Adoption, Search and Reunion by David Howe and Julia Feast, BAAF, 2003. *An investigation into why some adopted adults search for their birth parents, while others do not. Centres on the long-term experiences of 500 adults who were placed for adoption as children. See Appendix 2 for contact details.*

Adoption: What it is and what it means by Shaila Shah, BAAF, 2003. *A short, brightly illustrated guide to adoption for children and young people, which sets out information about the processes and procedures simply and clearly.*

'Adoption with contact: a study of adoptive parents and the impact of continuing contact with families of origin' by M. Sykes, *Adoption & Fostering*, 24:2, BAAF, 2000.

Adoptive Parents: Rights to leave and pay when a child is placed for adoption in the UK, Department for Transport and Industry. Publications order line: 0870 1502 500

Attachment Theory, Child Maltreatment and Family Support by David Howe *et al*, Macmillan, 1999. *Offers a comprehensive account of how social developmental perspectives and attachment theory can illuminate practice in the field of child protection and family support, drawing extensively on case study material.*

Attachment, Trauma and Healing: Understanding and treating attachment disorder in children and families by Terry M. Levy and Michael Orlans, Child Welfare League of America Press, 1998, USA. *Provides a detailed, but more clinically-based approach to attachment issues in children.*

Attachment, Trauma and Resilience: Therapeutic caring for children by Kate Cairns, BAAF, 2002. *Written by someone who cared for several children, this book provides an illustration of family life with children who have lived through overwhelming stress.*

Banished to the Exclusion Zone: School exclusion and the law Available from the Children's Legal Centre. *See Appendix 2 for contact details.*

Behind the Behaviour Available from Mental Health Media (Tel: 020 7700 8171). *A new video to help teachers understand the role they can play in children's mental health.*

Checklist for Prospective Adopters Available from Adoption UK. *Lists questions prospective adopters should consider and should discuss with their social worker at all stages of the adoption process.*

Children Adopted from Abroad: Key health and developmental issues, BAAF, 2004. *A pamphlet aimed at intercountry adopters, which explains and advises on possible child health problems and the screening of children adopted from overseas.*

Child and Adolescent Mental Health Services: Everybody's business National Assembly for Wales. Available from 029 2082 3480 or www.wales.gov.uk

Children Exposed to Parental Substance Misuse edited by Rena Phillips, BAAF, 2004. *This anthology looks at the effects on children of drugs, alcohol and other substances misused by parents, especially mothers during pregnancy. Contains invaluable tools, suggestions and resources.*

Child Adoption: A guidebook for adoptive parents and their advisors by Rene Hoksbergen, Jessica Kingsley Publishers, 1997. *A comprehensive guide written by the general director of the Adoption Centre at Utrecht University. Discusses many issues, including preparing for adoption, adopting children from different ethnic and cultural backgrounds, and helping the child adjust to school.*

Child Care Law: A summary of the law in England and Wales by Deborah Cullen and Mary Lane, BAAF, 2003. *Quick-reference guide to the law (in England and Wales) regarding the care of children.*

Child Care Law: Scotland by Alexandra Plumtree, BAAF, 1997. *Quick-reference guide to the law (in Scotland) regarding the care of children.*

The Children Act and the Courts: A guide for parents Available from the Department of Health. *A booklet that describes how the Children Act affects parents and children involved in court cases.*

The Children Act and Local Authorities: A guide for parents Available from the Department of Health. *A booklet that describes the Children Act, the role of local authorities, and what services and entitlements parents can expect as a result of the Act.*

Do You Know Someone Who Has Been Sexually Abused? Available from YoungMinds. *Produced specifically for parents. See Appendix 2 for contact details.*

Draw on Your Emotions: Creative ways to explore, express and understand important feelings by Margot Sunderland and Philip Engleheart, Speechmark Publishing Ltd., 1993. *A series of structured, easy picture exercises to help people of all ages express, communicate and deal more effectively with their emotions in everyday life. Designed for health professionals, but can be used by parents with their children.*
Tel: 01304 226900
email: orders@smallwood.co.uk

The Dynamics of Adoption: Social and personal perspectives edited by Amal Treacher and Ilan Katz, Jessica Kingsley, 2000. *A collection of essays about adoption.*

'Early adversity and adoptive solutions' by Ann and Alan Clarke, in *Adoption & Fostering*, 25:1, BAAF, 2001.

Effective Panels (2nd edn) by Jenifer Lord, Sylvia Barker and Deborah Cullen, BAAF, 2000. *Provides guidance on regulations, process and good practice in adoption and permanence panels.*

Facilitating Developmental Attachment: The road to emotional recovery and behavioral change in foster and adopted children by Daniel A. Hughes, Jason Aronson, Inc., 1997, USA. *An easy-to-read book written by a leading clinical psychologist in the U.S. who specialises in helping foster and adopted children and families. The book provides an in-depth look at attachment issues in children and provides many strategies for parents.*

'Family building in adoption' by B. Prynn, *Adoption & Fostering*, 25:1, 2001.

Finding a Way Through: Therapeutic caring for children Kate Cairns in conversation with John Simmonds, video, BAAF, 2003. *An inspirational and powerful video in which John Simmonds talks to Kate Cairns, author of* Attachment, Trauma and Resilience, *about being a parent/carer and how parents can help traumatised children to heal.*

First Steps in Parenting the Child Who Hurts: Tiddlers and toddlers by Caroline Archer, Jessica Kingsley, 1999. *Discusses the attachment and developmental issues that arise when even the youngest child is in your care.*

Fostering Attachments: Long-term outcomes in family group care by Brian Cairns, BAAF, 2004. *Describes the benefits of family group membership in aiding learning and recovery for children with difficult pasts.*

'Gay men and lesbians as adoptive parents' by G. Mallon, in *Journal of Gay and Lesbian Social Services*, 11:4, 2000.

How Can I Complain: Making a complaint to the Social Services Department Available from the Children's Legal Centre. *See Appendix 2 for contact details.*

Intercountry Adoption by Cherry Harnott, BAAF, 2004. *A pamphlet which describes the intercountry adoption process, issues and implications for families involved, and basic practical guidance on procedures and rules.*

Intercountry Adoption: Developments, trends and perspectives edited by Peter Selman, BAAF, 2000. *An anthology about several aspects of intercountry adoption as seen from diverse perspectives – parents, young people, researchers and practitioners.*

'Inviting applicants, birth parents and young people to attend adoption panel: how it works in practice' by S. Pepys and J. Dix, *Adoption & Fostering*, 24:4, BAAF, 2000.

Key Issues in Assessment: Points to consider when making decisions about applicants BAAF, 1998. *Provides advice to prospective adopters and foster carers who are beginning the formal assessment process.*

Learn the Child: Helping looked after children to learn by Kate Cairns and Chris Stanway, BAAF, 2004. *A resource pack, consisting of a book and CD ROM, which looks at the long-term effects of trauma in childhood and how this can affect learning, with suggestions for how traumatised children can best be supported by carers and professionals.*

Learning Disabilities in Children by Peter Burke and Katy Cigno, Blackwell Science, 2000. *Explains how learning difficulties are defined and examines their impact on family life. The book is aimed at those working in child welfare, social work and community care.*

Lesbian and Gay Fostering and Adoption: Extraordinary, yet ordinary edited by Stephen Hicks and Janet McDermott, Jessica Kingsley Publishers, 1999. *Diverse stories from lesbian and gay adopters and foster carers about caring for young children.*

Life Story Work by Tony Ryan and Rodger Walker, BAAF, 1999. *A popular guide that provides insight, ideas and exercises to use for life story work.*

Linking and Introductions: Helping children join adoptive families by Sheila Byrne, BAAF, 2001. *Provides useful practice guidance on the major stages of linking and introductions.*

Mental Health in Your School: A guide for teachers and others working in schools by Peter Wilson, YoungMinds, 1996, available from Jessica Kingsley (see below). *A practical and helpful guidebook.*

The Mental Health Needs of Looked After Children edited by Joanna Richardson and Carol Joughin, Gaskell, 2000. *Describes mental health problems of children in care. Written primarily for social workers and foster carers, this book emphasises the importance of prevention and early recognition of mental health problems.*

Modern Social Services: A commitment to people, the 9th Annual Report of the Chief Inspector of Social Services. Available free from Department of Health Publications, PO Box 777, London SE1 6XH.

My Life and Me by Jean Camis, BAAF, 2001. *A colourful and comprehensive life story workbook which will help children develop and record memories and recollections of their past and their birth family. With comprehensive guidelines for the adult working with the child.*

Neglect – A Fifty-Year Search for Answers edited by Mary Jean Pritchard. Available from The Bridge Publishing House (see below). *A collection of papers presented to a national conference. Contents include: 'Neglect: its effect on children and young people – an educational perspective'; 'Neglect: its effect on children and young people – a psychological perspective'; 'Neglect: a parental perspective'.*

Next Steps in Parenting the Child Who Hurts: Tykes and teens by Caroline Archer, Jessica Kingsley, 1999. *This book follows on logically from the First Steps book and continues into the challenging journey through childhood and into adolescence.*

Nobody Ever Told Us School Mattered: Raising the educational attainments of children in care edited by Sonia Jackson, BAAF, 2001. *An anthology that considers what can be done to ensure that looked after children have a better chance to succeed.*

Novices, Old Hands and Professionals: Adoption by single people by Morag Owen, BAAF, 1999. *Documents and comments on the experiences of single adopters and their children.*

Parents as Partners in the Treatment of Dissociative Children by Frances S. Waters, MSW, in *The Dissociative Child: Diagnosis, Treatment and Management* by J. Silberg, 1996, The Sidran Press. Text available on www.sidran.org/side13.html

The Patient's Charter: Services for children and young people produced by the Department of Health. Available by phoning the Health Literature Line, 0800 555 777. *Outlines the rights and standards for children's care within the NHS. (Note: Although still applicable to Wales and Scotland, in England the Patient's Charter was replaced by the Government's Health Plan for 2001.)*

The Placement of Children with Disabilities BAAF 1998. *Contains useful information for social workers, carers and parents about family placement of children with severe to profound disabilities.*

Preparing to Adopt: A training pack for preparation groups by Eileen Fursland, BAAF, 2002. *A training pack, consisting of a trainer's guide, an applicant's workbook and a video, designed to prepare prospective adopters for all the aspects of the adoption process.*

A Procedural Guide to Intercountry Adoption Available from the Overseas Adoption Helpline. *See Appendix 2 for contact details.*

Promoting Children's Mental Health within Early Years and School Settings Department for Education and Skills (DfES), 2001. *Provides examples of mental health initiatives taking place in schools and gives advice on helping children who have mental health problems or who have difficulties at school.*

Race and Ethnicity: A consideration of issues for black, minority ethnic and white children in family placement by Beverley Prevatt-Goldstein and Marcia Spencer, BAAF, 2000. *Includes research findings, and specific needs arising from children's racial origin, culture, religion and language.*

Related by Adoption: A handbook for grandparents and other relatives by Hedi Argent with a contribution from Kate Cairns, BAAF, 2004. *This brief and sensitively written handbook aims to give grandparents-to-be and other relatives information about adoption today and how the wider family can support building a family through adoption.*

Searching Questions: Identity, origins and adoption by Julia Feast and Terry Philpot, BAAF, 2003 (book and video). *Highlights the issues involved in searching and reunion. Designed for training, discussion groups or individuals who have been affected by these subjects.*

Siblings in Late Permanent Placements by Alan Rushton *et al*, BAAF, 2001. *A research study that explores the complexities of sibling placements.*

Special Education Handbook: The law on children with special needs Available from the Advisory Centre for Education. *Explains the process of obtaining a statement of special educational needs and various aspects of the statementing process. See Appendix 2 for contact details.*

Special Educational Needs: A guide for parents Department for Education and Skills (DfES). *See Appendix 2 for contact details.*

Special Educational Needs Update *A newsletter published by the Department for Education and Skills (DfES, see Appendix 2) and sent to all schools, local education authorities, health authorities, social services departments, and NHS Trusts in England.*

Special Needs: A guide for parents and carers of Jewish children with special educational needs Available from the Board of Deputies of British Jews, Tel: 020 7543 5400.

Special Schools in Britain, 2000/2001 National Association for Special Educational Needs (NASEN) *See Appendix 2 for contact details.*

Stories for Troubled Children by Margot Sunderland, Speechmark Publishing. *Five books to help children think about their feelings and to work through issues that trouble them.*
Willy and the Wobbly House *a story for children who are anxious or obsessional;*
A Wibble Called Biley (and a Few Honks) *a story for children who have hardened their hearts or who have become bullies;*
A Pea Called Mildred *to help children pursue their hopes and dreams;*
A Nifflenoo Called Nevermind *for children who bottle up their feelings;*
The Frog Who Longed for the Moon to Smile *for children who yearn for someone they love.*

Talking about Adoption to your Adopted Child by Marjorie Morrison, BAAF, 2004 (3rd edition). *A useful guide that advises how and when to explain to your child that he or she is adopted.*

Together or Apart? Assessing brothers and sisters for permanent placement by Jenifer Lord and Sarah Borthwick, BAAF, 2001. *Looks at the factors that should be considered in placing sibling groups.*

'Trauma experienced by children adopted from abroad' by R. Hoksbergen and C. van Dijkum, *Adoption & Fostering*, 25:2, 2001.

We Are Family: Sibling relationships in placement and beyond edited by Audrey Mullender, BAAF, 1999. *An anthology on various aspects of sibling relationships from diverse perspectives.*

Whatever happened to Adam? Stories of disabled people who were adopted or fostered by Hedi Argent, BAAF, 1998. *This remarkable book tells the stories of 20 young disabled people and the families who chose to care for them.*

What is a Disability? by Hedi Argent, BAAF, 2004. *A colourful and user-friendly children's guide which explains what disabilities are and what they can mean for those who have them.*

Books for children who have been adopted or fostered

Nutmeg Gets Adopted by Judith Foxon, illustrated by Sarah Rawlings, BAAF, 2001. *A story book for children, illustrated in full colour, which tells the story of Nutmeg, a little squirrel, and his younger sister and brother who go to live with a new family after their birth mother realises she cannot keep them safe. The series continues with* **Nutmeg Gets Cross** (2002) *in which Nutmeg learns to explore and understand his painful feelings about his adoption, and* **Nutmeg Gets a Letter** (2003), *which focuses on the issue of contact in adoption.* **Nutmeg Gets a Little Help** (forthcoming, 2004) *will look at post-adoption support and the ways in which this can help adopted children.*

Children's Book Series by Sheila Byrne and Leigh Chambers, illustrations by Sarah Rawlings, BAAF. *When children are separated from their birth families, part of their very self is in jeopardy. They need help to make sense of their experiences and individual history. This unique series of popular books for use with separated children is designed to do just that. Titles include:*
Joining together – Jo's story *A story about a step-parent adoption.*
Feeling safe – Tina's story *A story about a girl who has to go into foster care following abuse in the home.*
Living with a new family – Nadia and Rashid's story *A story about a brother and sister being adopted.*

Belonging doesn't mean forgetting – Nathan's story *A story about a four-year-old boy being adopted.*
Hoping for the best – Jack's story *A story about an adoption that did not work out.*

Chester and Daisy Move On by Angela Lidster, illustrations by Robyn Allpress, BAAF, 1995. *This engaging picture book is for use with children who are moving on to adoption. It tells the story of Chester and Daisy, two little bear cubs who have to leave their parents and live with a new bear family.*

Dennis Duckling: Going into care by Barbara Orritt, illustrations by David Thelwell, The Children's Society, 1999 (2nd edn). *This little book tells the story of Dennis, an appealing duckling, who has to leave his family as they can no longer look after him.*

Adoption: What it is and what it means by Shaila Shah, BAAF, 2003. *A short, colourful guide for children about the adoption process, including easy-to-understand definitions.*

What Happens in Court? by Hedi Argent, BAAF, 2003. *A colourful, user-friendly guide for children to help them understand the role a court might play in their lives, particularly if they have been or are going to be fostered or adopted.*

Publishers

(in addition to the organisations listed above and whose contact details are listed in Appendix 2, e.g. Adoption UK and BAAF)

Blackwell Publishing Ltd
Publishers of medicine, nursing, and life sciences titles.
9600 Garsington Road
Oxford OX4 2DQ
Tel: 01865 776 868
www.blackwellpublishing.com

The Bridge Publishing House Ltd
2 Cwm Cottages
Ciltwrch
Glasbury-on-Wye HR3 5NZ
Tel: 01497 847 094
email: info@bridgepublishing.co.uk
www.bridgepublishing.co.uk

David Fulton Publishers
Publishes a variety of books about behaviour management and mental health in children.
Titles include:
'Managing Attention Deficit/Hyperactivity Disorder in the Inclusive Classroom';
'Young Children and Classroom Behaviour';
'Supporting Pupils with Emotional Difficulties'; and
'Perspectives on Behaviour: A practical guide to interventions for teachers'.
The Chiswick Centre
412 Chiswick High Road
London W4 5TF
Tel: 0500 618 052
www.fultonpublishers.co.uk

Jessica Kingsley Publishers
Publishers of psychology, psychotherapy, psychiatry, social work and special needs publications.
116 Pentonville Road
London N1 9JB
Tel: 020 7833 2307
www.jkp.com

Pavilion

Provides training materials, publications, conferences and journals to those involved in health and social care.
The Ironworks
Cheapside
Brighton BN1 4ZZ
Tel: 01273 623 222
Fax: 01273 625 526
www.pavpub.com

Russell House Publishing

Produces a variety of books about social care issues and about parenting children who have been abused.
Some of their current titles include: 'The Foster Carer's Handbook';
'Strong Mothers: A resource for mothers and carers of children who have been sexually assaulted';
and a variety of titles for social services personnel.
Russell House Publishing Ltd.
4 St. George's House
The Business Park
Uplyme Road
Lyme Regis
Dorset DT7 3LS
Tel: 01297 443 948
email: help@russelhouse.co.uk
www.russelhouse.co.uk

SAGE Publications

Produces 'Emotional and Behavioural Difficulties', a quarterly research journal produced in association with the Association of Workers for Children with Emotional and Behavioural Difficulties (AWCEBD) (see Appendix 2). Available by subscription from the publisher.
SAGE Publications
1 Oliver's Yard
55 City Road
London EC1Y 1SP
Tel: 020 7374 0645
www.sagepub.co.uk

Speechmark Publications Ltd

Produces a series of books titled 'Helping Children with Feelings', designed to help children think about and deal with their emotions. There are five books in the series including: 'A Pea Called Mildred', 'Willy and the Wobbly House', and 'The Frog Who Longed for the Moon to Smile'.
Unit A11-A12
Telford Road
Bicester
Oxon OX26 4LQ
Tel: 0800 243 755
www.speechmark.net

Wiley Europe Ltd

Produces medicine, science and psychology publications.
The Atrium
Southern Gate
Chichester
West Sussex PO19 8SQ
Tel: 01243 779 777
www.wiley.co.uk

Journals and magazines

Adoption and Fostering *Quarterly journal of BAAF. Presents current issues in practice, policy, law and research in foster care and adoption throughout the UK. For anyone involved in foster care and adoption. Available by subscription from BAAF (see Appendix 2).*

Adoption Today *Bi-monthly magazine of Adoption UK. Directed mainly at people who have adopted or who are considering adoption. Part I of the magazine includes articles, news items, letters and book reviews about adoption. Part II of the magazine, Children Who Wait, provides information about children currently waiting to be adopted. The magazine is free with membership in Adoption UK (see Appendix 2).*

Be My Parent *Monthly UK-wide family-finding newspaper published by BAAF. Subscribers to Be My Parent include approved adopters, those waiting to be approved and those who have only just begun to think about adopting or permanently fostering. Over 300 children of all ages and with a wide range of needs from all over the country are featured each month. Available by subscription from BAAF (see Appendix 2).*

Appendix 2

Organisations, government agencies, websites

Organisations, services and government agencies

ADDISS (The National Attention Deficit Disorder Information and Support Service)
Provides information and resources about ADHD for parents, teachers and health professionals. In addition to publications, ADDISS resources include conferences, training and local support groups.
The ADDISS Resource Centre
10 Station Road
Mill Hill
London NW7 2JU
Tel: 020 8906 9068
email: resources@addiss.co.uk
email: info@addiss.co.uk
www.addiss.co.uk

ADD/ADHD Family Support Group UK
Send an s.a.e. for information to:
1a High Street, Dilton Marsh
Westbury, Wiltshire BA13 4DL
Enquire at:
209 – 211 City Road
London EC1V 1JN
Tel: 0808 808 3555
email: jim@cafamily.org.uk
www.cafamily.org.uk

ADHD UK Alliance
Publishes the newsletter, 'ADDvance'. Membership is free for parents and support groups.
Enquire at:
209 – 211 City Road
London EC1V 1JN
Tel: 020 7608 8760
email: jim@cafamily.org.uk
www.cafamily.org.uk

Adoption Register for England and Wales
Norwood Ravenswood
Broadway House, 80/82 Broadway
Stanmore, Middlesex HA7 4HB
Tel: 020 8420 6814

Adoption UK
A UK-wide self-help group run by adoptive parents who offer support before, during and after adoption. Services include a helpline; magazine that includes details of children waiting for adoption; and a variety of printed information about all aspects of adoption.
Manor Farm, Appletree Road
Chipping Warden, Banbury
Oxfordshire OX17 1LH
Helpline: 0870 770 0450
Administration: 01295 660 121
www.adoptionuk.org.uk

Adoptive Parents Association of Ireland
Glendalough Post Office
County Wicklow, Ireland
Tel: 00 35 3404 45184

Advisory Centre for Education (ACE)
Provides information about all aspects of state education and helps parents who are dealing with schools or education authorities.
Unit 1C, Aberdeen Studios
22 Highbury Grove, London N5 2EA
General advice line: 0808 800 5793
"Exclusion" advice line: 0808 800 0327
www.ace-ed.org.uk

After Adoption
Tel: 0800 0568 578 (for service users)
0161 839 493 (for professionals)
Full time offices:
Head Office
Canterbury House
12 – 14 Chapel Street
Manchester M3 7NH
North East Office
2nd Floor, Aiden House
Tynegate Business Centre
Sunderland Road
Gateshead NE8 3HU
Merseyside Office
60 Duke Street
Liverpool L1 5AA

Main Wales Office (South Wales)
2nd Floor, Dominion House North
Dominion Arcade
Queen Street
Cardiff CF10 2AR
Swansea Office
Swansea YMCA
1 The Kingsway
Swansea SA1 5JQ
London Office
85 Moorgate
London EC2M 6SA
Preston Office
Fishergate House
16 Walton Parade
Preston PR1 8QT
Part time offices:
West Wales
1st Floor, Agricultural House
Cambrian Place
Carmarthen SA31 1QG
Gwent Office
Torfaen People's Centre
Trosnant House
Trosnant Street
Pontypool
Torfaen NP4 8AT
North Wales
PO Box 52
Oswestry SY10 7ZT

Anna Freud Centre
A research and treatment centre for children and young people who have a range of emotional, behavioural and developmental difficulties. Information about its services, as well as summaries of research into attachment and other emotional/behavioural difficulties are provided on its website.
21 Maresfield Gardens
London NW3 5SD
Tel: 020 7794 2313
www.annafreudcentre.org

Association for Child Psychology and Psychiatry

An association for professionals of various disciplines who are involved with children. It arranges seminars and publishes professional journals. It does not provide an advice service.
39 – 41 Union Street, London SE1 1SD
Tel: 020 7403 7458
www.acpp.org.uk

Association for Families who have Adopted from Abroad (AFAA)

Provides information about various aspects of international adoption to prospective adopters, adoptive families, social services and the media.
30 Bradgate
Cuffley EN6 4RL
Tel: 01707 878 793
email: information.afaa@ntlworld.com
www.afaa.org.uk

Association of Child Psychotherapists (ACP)

Maintains register of accredited child psychotherapists and gives details of local child psychotherapists.
120 West Heath Road
London NW3 7TU
Tel: 020 8458 1609
email: inquiries@acp.uk.net
www.acp.uk.net

Association of Transracially Adopted People (ATRAP)

Supports transracially adopted or fostered people. Provides quarterly newsletter, monthly social meetings, informal support and social network, events and a bulletin by email for members.
Has moved, no current information

Benefit Enquiry Line
Tel: 0800 220 674

Birthlink (formerly Family Care Birthlink)

They offer post-adoption counselling and run Scotland's only contact register. Publish 'Relatively Unknown' which has short stories about Scottish adoption.
21 Castle Street
Edinburgh EH2 3DN
Tel: 0131 225 6441
www.birthlink.org.uk

British Association for Adoption and Fostering (BAAF)

UK-wide membership organisation for agencies and individuals concerned with adoption and fostering. Provides publications for adopters, social work practitioners and other professionals, and a family-finding service, 'Be My Parent'. Also provides information and advice, and organises conferences and seminars. Offices in England, Scotland and Wales.
Skyline House, 200 Union Street
London SE1 0LX
Tel: 020 7593 2000
www.baaf.org.uk

British Association for Counselling and Psychotherapy (BACP)

Send SAE for details of local counsellors and psychotherapists.
BACP House
35 – 37 Albert Street
Rugby
Warwickshire CV21 2SG
Tel: 0870 443 5252
Monday – Friday 9.30am – 3pm
(information)
email: bacp@bacp.co.uk
www.bacp.co.uk

The British Association of Psychotherapists (BAP)

The training and professional institution of psychoanalytic psychotherapists, analytical psycholoists (Jungian) and child psychotherapists.
37 Mapesbury Road
London NW2 4HJ
Tel: 020 8452 9823
www.bap-psychotherapy.org

British Institute for Learning Disabilities (BILD)

Services include information about various learning disabilities, resources, conferences and events. Also supports research into learning disabilities.
Campion House, Green Street
Kidderminster, Worcestershire DY10 1JL
Tel: 01562 723 010
www.bild.org.uk

Caspari Foundation (formerly Forum for Educational Therapy and Therapeutic Teaching, FAETT)

Dedicated to promoting educational therapy and therapeutic learning to help children who have emotional barriers that can impair learning. Organises lectures and events.
Caspari House, 1 Noel Road
London N1 8HQ
Tel: 020 7704 1977
www.caspari.org.uk

Catholic Children's Society (Nottingham)
7 Colwick Road
Nottingham NG2 5FR
Tel: 0115 955 8811
email: enquiries@ccsnotts.co.uk
www.ccsnotts.co.uk

The Centre for Child Mental Health

Promotes awareness of the emotional well-being and mental health of children. Disseminates research to health professionals, parents and the media through conferences, publications and workshops.
2 – 18 Britannia Row
London N1 8PA
Tel: 020 7354 2913
email: info@childmentalhealthcentre.org
www.childmentalhealthcentre.org

Child Psychotherapy Trust

Provides information about children's emotional development and behaviour; promotes understanding of child psychotherapy and access to child psychotherapy services; supports training of child psychotherapists.
Star House, 104 – 108 Grafton Road
London NW5 4BD
Tel: 020 7284 1355
Helpline: 020 7485 5510
www.childpsychotherapytrust.org.uk

Children and Family Courts Advisory and Support Service (CAFCASS)

Service provided by practitioners (including children's guardians) who advise courts about the well-being of children and their families. The website provides general information about CAFCASS, publications, and links to related sites.
8th Floor, Wyndham House
189 Marsh Wall
London E14 9SH
Tel: 020 7510 7000
www.cafcass.gov.uk

Children in Scotland

Provides a national information and advice service, Enquire, for parents, professionals, children and young people who have questions about special educational needs.
5 Shandwick Place
Edinburgh EH2 4RG
Helpline: 0845 123 2303
www.childreninscotland.org.uk

The Children's Legal Centre

An independent national charity concerned with law and policy affecting children and young people. Produces a monthly journal, 'childRight', as well as information sheets and booklets. In addition to policy and campaign work, CLC also provides an advice and information service (free and confidential legal advice), as well as the Education Legal Advocacy Unit, which provides advice and representation to children and/or parents involved in education disputes with a school or local education authority.
The Children's Legal Centre
University of Essex, Wivenhoe Park
Colchester CO4 3SQ
Administration and publications:
01206 872 466
National education line: 0845 345 4345
www.childrenslegalcentre.com

The Children's Society

UK-wide charity which provides projects and information for families who are experiencing difficulties.
Edward Rudolf House, Margery Street
London WC1X 0JL
Tel: 020 7841 4415
www.the-childrens-society.org.uk

Commission for Social Care Inspection (CSCI)

Responsible for inspecting and registering adoption and fostering services in England.
33 Greycoat Street
London SW1P 2QF
Tel: 020 7979 2000/0845 015 0120
www.csci.org.uk

Community Legal Service

A government initiative designed to ensure everyone has access to quality legal advice and information. The service can be provided by CABs, solicitors' firms and legal advice centres that have been awarded the Community Legal Service Quality mark. You can find the 'Community Legal Service Directory' at your local library. It lists all law firms and advice centres that have the Quality Mark, and indicates whether firms offer free advice or if they charge for advice.

The Community Legal Service website, www.clsdirect.org.uk, provides the 'Community Legal Service Directory', legal information and advice, and links to websites for other advice organisations.
Tel: 0845 345 4345 for information about CLS providers or about the CLS directory.

Connexions

New service providing advice and support for young people (aged 13 –19) in England, with priority given to young people who are '…at greatest risk of not making a successful transition to adulthood'. A network of Connexions advisers helps young people with decisions about life, education and careers. There are 47 local partnerships to contact on the website:
www.connexions.gov.uk

Contact a Family

Provides information for parents on over 2,000 rare medical conditions, including information about support groups, and publishes a useful directory, 'The CAF Directory of Specific Conditions and Rare Disorders – 2002'. There is also a freephone helpline for parents seeking information regarding help for disabled children.
209 –211 City Road, London EC1V 1JN
Helpline: 0808 808 3555
Monday – Friday 10am – 4pm
Tel: 020 7608 8700
email: jim@cafamily.org.uk
www.cafamily.org.uk

Contact Register for England and Wales

The General Register Office
Adoption Section
Smedley Hydro, Trafalgar Road
Southport, Merseyside PR8 2HH
Tel: 0151 471 4831
email: admin@adoptionregister.net
www.adoptionregister.net

ContinYou (formerly Special Education Consortium)

Unit C1, Grovelands Court
Grovelands Estate
Lonford Road
Exhall
Coventry CV7 9NE
Tel: 0247 658 8440
email: info.coventry@continyou.org.uk
www.cedc.org.uk

Council for Disabled Children

Promotes collaborative work between different organisations providing services and support for children and young people with disabilities and special educational needs. Offers a range of services including consultancy, training, information, publications and conferences.
8 Wakley Street, London EC1
Tel: 020 7843 1900
email: cdc@ncb.org.uk
www.ncb.org.uk/cdc/index

The Court Service

Clive House
Petty France
London SW1H 9HD
Tel: 020 7189 2000
www.courtservice.gov.uk

DDAT (UK) Ltd (formerly Dyslexia, Dyspraxia and Attention Treatment Centre)

Provides assessment, consultation and treatment for children, adolescents and adults who may have dyslexia, dyspraxia or attention difficulties. Contact the Centre for further information about its services and its fees.
Camden House
Warwick Road
Kenilworth CV8 1TH
Tel: 0870 737 0017/0870 880 6060
email: info@ddat.co.uk
www.ddat.co.uk

Department for Education and Skills (DfES)

Provides information for parents about all aspects of education and schools. The DfES website offers a Parents' Centre that provides specific and comprehensive information about SEN. Contact the DfES publications department to find out about specific information for parents, such as the 'SEN Guide for Parents', and for a copy of the 'Code of Practice'.
DfES Publications
PO Box 5050, Annesley
Nottingham NG15 0DL
Tel: 0845 602 2260/020 7972 2000
Adoption Helpline: 020 7972 4014
10am – 12noon
Fax: 0845 603 3360
email: dfes@prolog.uk.com
www.dfes.gov.uk/adoption
www.parentcentre.gov.uk

Department of Health Publications

PO Box 777
London SE1 6XH
Tel: 08701 555 455
Fax: 01623 724 524
email: doh@prolog.uk.com

Depression Alliance
Promotes greater understanding of depression to reduce the stigma associated with it. Produces a free booklet, 'The Young Person's Guide to Stress'.
35 Westminster Bridge Road
London SE1 7JB
Tel: 0845 123 2320
www.depressionalliance.org

Family Futures Consortium Ltd
A service for families who adopt or foster. Provides an assessment service and also an intensive attachment programme. Also seminars and training programmes for parents, carers and social workers to help support families and children.
35A Britannia Row
Islington
London N1 8QH
Tel: 020 7354 4161
email: contact@familyfutures.co.uk
www.familyfutures.co.uk

Family Rights Group (FRG)
A national organisation that advises families who are in contact with social services, about the care of their children.
The Print House, 18 Ashwin Street
London E8 3DL
Tel: 0800 731 1696
www.frg.org.uk

Fostering Network (formerly NFCA)
Provides support and information for foster carers to ensure that all children who are fostered receive the highest standards of care.
87 Blackfriars Road, London SE1 8HA
Tel: 020 7620 6400
www.fostering.net
Scotland office
2nd Floor, Ingram House
227 Ingram Street, Glasgow G1 1DA
Tel: 0141 204 1400
www.fostering.net

Gay Dads Group
Tel: 020 7681 7425
email: hmlondon@blueyonder.co.uk

The General Register Office for Scotland
New Register House, Edinburgh EH1 7YT
Tel: 0131 334 0380
www.gro-scotland.gov.uk

General Registrar Office Northern Ireland
Oxford House
49 – 55 Chichester Street
Belfast BT1 4HL
Tel: 028 9025 2000
www.groni.gov.uk

General Social Care Council (GSCC)
Regulatory body for the social care profession in England.
Goldings House, Hay's Galleria
London SE1
Tel: 020 7397 5100
www.gscc.org.uk

Health Quality Services (HQS)
Runs accreditation schemes for health services, and is developing a quality accreditations scheme for child and adolescent mental health services.
15 Whitehall
London SW1A 2DD
ww.hqs.org.uk

Her Majesty's Stationery Office (HMSO)
St Clement's House, 2 – 16 Colegate
Norwich NR3 1BQ
www.hmso.gov.uk
and
The Stationery Office
PO Box 29, Norwich NR3 1GN
Tel: 0870 600 5522 (general enquiries)
     0845 702 3474 (copies of legislation)

Home Education Advisory Service (HEAS)
A UK-based national charity providing information and support for home education. Produces information, provides support for parents, works with LEAs to monitor and inspect home education programmes.
PO Box 98, Welwyn Garden City
Hertfordshire AL8 6AN
Tel: 01707 371 854
email: admin@heas.org.uk
www.heas.org.uk

Independent Panel for Special Education Advice (IPSEA)
A volunteer-based organisation that aims to ensure that children with special educational needs receive the special education provision to which they are legally entitled. Provides free, independent advice; free advice on appealing to the Special Educational Needs Tribunal (including representation, if needed); second opinions from professionals.
6 Carlow Mews, Woodbridge
Suffolk IP12 1DH
Advice line: Monday – Tuesday
10am – 4pm and 6 – 7pm
0800 018 4016 or 01394 380 518
Scotland: 0131 665 4396
Northern Ireland: 01232 705 654
Tribunal appeals only: 01394 384 711
www.ipsea.org.uk

Independent Review Mechanism (IRM)
Dolphin House, 54 Coventry Road
Birmingham B10 0RX
Tel: 0121 766 8086
email: irm@baaf.org.uk
www.irm-adoption.org.uk

The Institute for Arts in Therapy and Education
A college of higher education dedicated to in-depth theoretical and practical study of artistic, imaginative and emotional expression and understanding and enhancement of emotional well-being.
2 – 18 Britannia Row, London N1 8PA
Tel: 020 7704 2534
email: info@arts-therapy.demon.co.uk
www.artspsychotherapy.co.uk

The Institute for Neuro-phsyiological Psychology
Established in 1975 to research the effects of central nervous system dysfunction on learning difficulties in children and on adults suffering from neuroses. The institute provides detailed information about this topic and about its services on its website or via post.
Warwick House, 1 Stanley Street
Chester CH1 2LR
Tel: 01244 311 414
www.inpp.org.uk

Institute of Child Health
Works in partnership with the Great Ormond Street Hospital to form the largest paediatric training and research centre in the UK. The hospital offers the widest range of paediatric specialists in the country.
30 Guildford Street, London WC1N 1EH
Tel: 020 7242 9789
www.ich.ucl.ac.uk

Intercountry Adoption (formerly Intercountry Adoption Lawyers Association)
Buryfields House
Buryfields
Guildford GU2 4AZ
Tel: 01483 252 525

International Foster Care Organisation (IFCO)
A voluntary organisation committed to improving the quality of service for children in care, and for developing standards for organisations and individual carers. Services include international and regional conferences, a newsletter, and various projects.
Anna Paulownastraat 103
2518 BC The Hague
The Netherlands
email: denhaagoffice@ifco.info
www.ifco.info
www.internationalfostering.org

International Social Service UK
A voluntary organisation that helps families and individuals whose lives are split between different countries.
3rd Floor, Cranmer House
39 Brixton Road, London SW9 6DD
Tel: 020 7735 8941
email: mark.issuk@btopenworld.com
www.issuk.org.uk

Jewish Association for Fostering, Adoption and Infertility (JAFA)
Tel: 020 8207 6585

Lesbian and Gay Foster and Adoptive Parents Network
c/o Stonewall Parenting
46 Grosvenor Gardens
London SW1W 0EB
Tel: 020 7881 9440
email: info@stonewall.org.uk
www.stonewall.org.uk

LifeBytes
A health website for young people (aged 11–14) that provides health education, but not health advice. Produced by the Department of Health and the Health Education Authority.
www.lifebytes.gov.uk

The Mental Health Foundation
Provides information and support for people and families who have any type of mental health problem and/or learning disability. Included within the MHF is 'The Foundation for People with Learning Disabilities'.
7th Floor, 83 Victoria Street
London SW1H 0HW
Tel: 020 7802 0300
email: mhf@mhf.org.uk
www.mentalhealth.org.uk
Scotland office:
5th Floor, Merchants House
30 George Square, Glasgow G2 1EG
Tel: 0141 572 0145
email: scotland@mhf.org.uk
www.mentalhealth.org.uk
www.learningdisabilities.org.uk

Mentality
The national charity dedicated to the promotion of mental health. Provides a range of services and resources, policy work, campaigning and practical work. Has experience working with children who are looked after, away from home.
134 – 138 Borough High Street
London SE1 1LB
Tel: 020 7716 6777
email: enquiries@mentality.org.uk
www.mentality.org.uk

National Association for Special Educational Needs (NASEN)
Promotes the education, training, advancement and development of people with special educational needs. Services to members include several regular publications, and regional courses and conferences.
4 – 5 Amber Business Village
Amber Close, Amington
Tamworth B77 4RP
Tel: 01827 311 500
email: welcome@nasen.org.uk
www.nasen.org.uk

National Children's Bureau
Promotes the well-being of children in every aspect of life. Participates in research and policy development, and provides an information service, publications and training.
8 Wakley Street, London EC1V 7QE
Tel: 020 7843 6000
Children in Scotland
Tel: 0131 228 8484
Children in Wales
Tel: 029 2034 2434
www.ncb.org.uk

National Family and Parenting Institute
Supports parents in bringing up children and promotes the well-being of families. Services include publications and conferences.
430 Highgate Studios
53 – 79 Highgate Road
London NW5 1TL
Tel: 020 7424 3460
email: info@nfpi.org
www.nfpi.org

NORCAP – supporting adults affected by adoption
Provides information, support and counselling services including for those wishing to trace birth relatives.
112 Church Road, Wheatley
Oxfordshire OX33 1LU
Tel: 01865 875 000
email: enquiries@norcap.org.uk
www.norcap.org.uk

National Society for the Prevention of Cruelty to Children (NSPCC)
Provides information and training, in addition to campaign and policy work to prevent abuse of children.
Weston House, 42 Curtain Road
London EC2A 3NH
Tel: 020 7825 2500
Helpline: 0808 800 5000
www.nspcc.org.uk

Our Place
A registered charity that provides support for families who foster or adopt. Offers workshops, activities, consultations, networking opportunities.
139 Fishponds Road
Eastville, Bristol BS5 6PR
Tel: 0117 951 2433
email: ourplace1@btconnect.com

Overseas Adoption Helpline
A confidential information and advice service for intercountry adopters at any stage of adoption or post adoption. Services include an advice line; counselling for families or for young people who were adopted from over-seas; training for professionals involved in adoption; and 'consultation days' for prospective intercountry adopters.
64 – 66 High Street, Barnet
Hertfordshire EN5 5SJ
Tel: 0870 516 8742
email: info@oah.org.uk
www.oah.org.uk

Overseas Adoption Support and Information Service (OASIS)
A self-help group that provides information and advice for intercountry adopters, as well as post-adoption support. Produces leaflets and a newsletter, operates an advice line and conducts seminars.
14 Ashdowne Avenue
Saltdean
Brighton BN2 8AH
Tel: 0870 241 7069
www.adoptionoverseas.org.uk

Parentline Plus
Confidential helpline provides information and emotional support to parents.
Tel: 0808 800 2222
Textphone: 0800 783 6783
www.parentlineplus.co.uk

Positive Parenting Publications and Programmes
Provides information, resources and training for parents and those who support them.
2A South Street, Gosport
Hampshire PO12 1ES
Tel: 023 9252 8787
email:info@parenting.org.uk
www.parenting.org.uk

Project for Advocacy, Counselling and Education (PACE)
Offers support, information and training for lesbian and gay partners and individuals considering or involved in adoption.
34 Hartham Road
London N7 9JL
Tel: 020 7700 1323

School Health Service

Identifies and assesses children who have physical, emotional or behavioural problems. It includes a named school nurse and paediatric doctors who have additional training to help with school services. The Health Service provides advice to LEAs and offers specialist services, such as enuresis (bedwetting) clinics, audiology services, and support/advice for families and children with physical and emotional difficulties. Contact your local authority or LEA to find phone numbers for your local School Health Teams.

Scottish Health on the Web (SHOW)

Provided by the NHS in Scotland, this site provides general health information, contact details of all NHS Trusts, and links to other websites.
www.show.scot.nhs.uk

Social, Emotional and Behavioural Difficulties Association (SEBDA)

Promotes services for children and young people who have emotional and behavioural difficulties, and supports professionals working with young people. Produces journal, 'Emotional and Behavioural Difficulties', that provides a variety of articles written mainly by professionals in the field. The journal is available from SAGE Publications (see Appendix 1 for contact details). Also inhouse/membership paper 'Sebda News'.
SEBDA Head office
Church House
1 St. Andrew's View
Penrith
Cumbria CA11 7YF
Tel: 01768 210 510
email: admin@sebda.org
www.awcebd.co.uk

Special Education Consortium

See contact details for Council for Disabled Children.

TalkAdoption

A free, confidential national helpline for young people (to 25 years old) who have a link with adoption, whether adoptee, friend or relative.
Tuesday – Friday 3 – 9 pm
Tel: 0808 808 1234
www.talkadoption.org.uk

The Who Cares? Trust

Promotes services for children and young people in public care and those who have left public care. Publishes 'Who Cares?' magazine quarterly.
Kemp House
152 – 160 City Road
London EC1V 2NP
Tel: 020 7251 3117
email: mailbox@thewhocarestrust.org.uk
www.thewhocarestrust.org.uk

Trust for the Study of Adolescence (TSA Ltd)

Aims to improve the lives of young people through research, training, development and publications. Focuses on disseminating information through conferences, training programmes and publications, especially in the areas of emotional well-being, health, parenting, family life, social action and youth justice.
23 New Road, Brighton BN1 1WZ
Tel: 01273 693 311
www.tsa.uk.com

UK Youth

A network of local providers of youth services. Delivers and supports high-quality voluntary work and informal education for young people. Provides publications for young people and youth workers about emotional/behavioural issues.
2nd Floor, Kirby House
20 – 24 Kirby Street
London EC1N 8TS
Tel: 020 7242 4045
email: info@ukyouth.org
www.ukyouth.org

United Kingdom Council for Psychotherapy (UKCP)

Holds national register of psychotherapists and gives details of local psychotherapists and counsellors.
167 – 169 Great Portland Street
London W1N 5FB
Tel: 020 7436 3002
email:ukcp@psychotherapy.org.uk
www.ukcp.org.uk

Warwickshire Parent Partnership Service (formerly National Parent Partnership Service)

Provides support for parents of children with special educational needs, via telephone contact, home visits or school meetings. Staff liaise with schools, LEA officers and Special Educational Needs Support Services. It organises regular meetings for parents; offers workshops to schools and governors, and to health and social services providers. Contact the National Parent Partnership Service for information about your local service.
c/o ContinYou
Unit C1, Grovelands Court
Grovelands Estate, Lonford Road, Exhall
Coventry CV7 9NE
Tel: 024 7658 8440
email: pps@cedc.org.uk

YoungMinds: the children's mental health charity

The national charity committed to improving the mental health of all children and young people. Produces a variety of information about many mental health issues, including 'YoungMinds Magazine'. Provides a consultancy service; works with health, education and social services, and the voluntary sector to develop services for children with mental health problems.
102 – 108 Clerkenwell Road
London EC1M 5SA
Tel: 020 7336 8445
email: info@youngminds.org.uk
www.youngminds.org.uk

YoungMinds Parents' Information Service

A telephone service providing information and advice for anyone with concerns about the mental health of a child or young person.
Helpline: 0800 018 2138
www.youngminds.org.uk/pis

Youth Access

Provides details of local, free and confidential youth counselling and information centres throughout the UK.
1A Taylors Yard, 67 Alderbrook Road
London SW12 8AD
Tel: 020 8772 9900
email: admin@youthaccess.org.uk
www.youthaccess.org.uk

Adoption agencies

Please refer to: **Adopting a Child**, available from BAAF, see p.97.

Post-adoption and adoption support services

Please see Section 5 of this handbook.

Websites

Adoption Information

Adopting.org
US-based site that, among other services, provides information and resources about general adoption issues.
www.adopting.org

Adoption & Fostering Information Line
An online service that provides links to sources of information about adoption. Administers LondonKIDS, a joint project by 23 London boroughs to recruit more foster carers and adoptive parents.
204 Stockport Road
Altrincham WA15 7UA
Tel: 0800 783 4086
www.adoption.org.uk
www.fostering.org.uk

Adoption Link UK
Formed to meet the needs of people separated from their birth families through adoption and who want to search for their birth family.
99 Claremont Avenue
Maghull
Liverpool L31 8AH
Tel: 0151 527 2218
email: info@adoptionlink.co.uk
www.adoptionlink.co.uk

Adoptions Together
A US-based site operated by the Center for Adoptive Families. Provides information and resources about many adoption issues.
www.adoptionstogether.org

Adoptshop.com
US-based site selling adoption-related items.
www.adoptionshop.com

Department for Education and Skills adoption website
www.dfes.gov.uk/adoption

LondonKIDS
Provided as part of a joint project by 23 London boroughs to recruit more adopters and foster carers. The site provides information and various features about adoption.
www.londonkids.org.uk

National Adoption Information Clearinghouse
A US organisation whose website provides an extensive list of organisations, publications about adoption, as well as links to other websites associated with adoption.
www.naic.acf.hhs.gov/

Pact: An adoption alliance
A US-based site that provides, among other services, resources and information about adoption. Focuses on support for adopted children and adults of color.
email: info@pactadopt.org
www.pactadopt.org

Parent Network for the Post-Institutionalized Child
A US-based site devoted to 'understanding the medical, developmental, emotional and educational needs of children adopted from hospital, orphanages and institutions throughout the world'.
www.pnpic.org

Raising Adopted Children
A US-based site that provides information about adoption-related issues.
www.raisingadoptedchildren.com

Education

Department for Education and Skills (DfES)
Standards website
Provides links to various government initiatives for raising standards in education, and provides a database of good practice programmes throughout the country.
www.standards.dfes.gov.uk
Special Educational Needs
DfES site with resources and information about special educational needs.
www.dfes.gov.uk/sen
Parents' site
Information and resources especially for parents.
www.parentcentre.gov.uk

Legal Advice

Compact Law
Provides specific information about adoption law.
www.compactlaw.co.uk

The Court Service
Clive House
Petty France
London SW1H 9HD
Tel: 020 7189 2000
www.courtservice.gov.uk

Family Solicitors
Provides advice; specific information about adoption; lists solicitors who specialise in adoption and other aspects of family law.
www.family-solicitors.co.uk

Lawrights
A legal and information service that provides specific information about adoption law.
www.lawrights.co.uk/adopt

Health and mental health

ATTACh
A US organisation that specialises in issues about the assessment and treatment of attachment difficulties.
email: info@attach.org
www.ATTACh.org

Attachment Home Page
A US-based site dedicated to helping parents and children develop strong attachments and bonds. Provides information and support about attachment difficulties.
www.attach-bond.com

Cascade Center for Family Growth
email: cascade@attachment.org

Center for Positive Behavioral Interventions and Support
Created by the US Department of Education to help schools implement and sustain positive behaviour-intervention programmes.
www.pbis.org

Council for Children with Behavioral Disorders (CCBD)
A US organisation that promotes education and the general welfare of children and youth who have emotional and behavioural disorders. Publishes a research journal, 'Behavioral Disorders', as well as a newsletter and a magazine.
www.ccbd.net

Department of Health
Database of good practice.
www.dh.gov.uk

Federation of Families for Children's Mental Health (FFCMH)
A US parent-run organisation that provides support and information for families of children and youth who have emotional, behavioural or mental disorders.
www.ffcmh.org

Internet Mental Health
General mental health information from the US.
email: internetmentalhealth@telus.net
www.mentalhealth.com

Mentality
Site to share ideas about mental health promotion. Operated by Mentality, a charity dedicated to the promotion of mental health.
email: enquiries@mentality.org.uk
www.mentality.org.uk

New York University Child Study Center
Provides comprehensive information about all aspects of child mental health, including information about various conditions, medications and research.
www.childmentalhealth.com

The Problem Child Website
A US-based site initiated by parents raising children with emotional/behavioural problems. Provides information and resources about many issues, including Attention Deficit/Hyperactivity Disorder, attachment difficulties, Asperger's Syndrome, learning difficulties and bedwetting.
www.problemchild.org

Psychiatry 24x7
Provides general mental health information.
www.psychiatry24x7.com

Radkid.org
A US-based site with information specifically about attachment difficulties sometimes referred to in the US as Reactive Attachment Disorder (RAD)
www.radkid.org

The Theraplay Institute
US-based site provided by the Theraplay Institute. Theraplay is therapist-directed play therapy for children and their parents, designed to 'enhance attachment, raise self-esteem, improve trust in others and create joyful engagement'.
www.theraplay.org

UK Health Centre
A general interest health resources library.
www.healthcentre.org.uk

Wired for Health
Addresses general health needs of school-age children and provides links to local and national information.
www.wiredforhealth.gov.uk

Appendix 3

National Adoption Standards for England

A. Children

The needs and wishes, welfare and safety of the looked after child are at the centre of the adoption process.

1. Children whose birth family cannot provide them with a secure, stable and permanent home are entitled to have adoption considered for them;

2. Whenever plans for permanence are being considered, they will be made on the basis of the needs of each looked after child; and within the following timescales;

   a) The child's need for a permanent home will be addressed at the four-month review and a plan for permanence made;

   b) Clear timescales will be set for achieving the plan, which will be appropriately monitored and considered at every subsequent review;

   c) Where adoption has been identified as the plan for the child at a review, the adoption panel will make its recommendation within 2 months.

Where adoption is the plan:

3. The timescales below will be followed, taking account of the individual child's needs:

   a) A match with suitable adoptive parents will be identified and approved by panel within 6 months of the agency agreeing that adoption is in the child's best interest;

   b) In care proceedings, where the plan is adoption, a match with suitable adoptive parents will be identified and approved by panel within 6 months of the court's decision;

   c) Where a parent has requested that a child aged under 6 months be placed for adoption, a match with suitable adoptive parents will be identified and approved by panel within 3 months of the agency agreeing that adoption is in the child's best interest.

4. Every child will have his or her wishes and feelings listened to, recorded and taken into account. Where they are not acted upon, the reasons for not doing so will be explained to the child and properly recorded.

5. All children will have a named social worker who will be responsible for them throughout the adoption process.

6. Children will be given clear explanations and information about adoption, covering what happens at each stage (including at court), and how long each stage is likely to take in their individual case.

7. Children will be well prepared before joining a new family. This will include clear appropriate information on their birth family and life before adoption, and information about the adopters and their family. Children are entitled to information provided by their birth families, which will be kept safe both by agencies and adopters. It will be provided to adopted children, or adults, at a time and in a manner that reflects their age and understanding, as well as the nature of the information concerned.

8. Children will be matched with families who can best meet their needs. They will not be left waiting indefinitely for a 'perfect family'.

9. Every effort will be made to recruit sufficient adopters from diverse backgrounds, so that each child can be found an adoptive family within the timescales in 3) above, which best meets their needs, and in particular:

   a) which reflects their ethnic origin, cultural background, religion and language;

   b) which allows them to live with brothers and sisters unless this will not meet their individually assessed needs. Where this is the case, a clear explanation will be given to them and recorded.

10. The child's needs, wishes and feelings, and their welfare and safety are the most important concerns when considering links or contact with birth parents, wider birth family members and other people who are significant to them.

11. Adoption plans will include details of the arrangements for maintaining links (including contact) with birth parents, wider birth family members and other people who are significant to the child and how and when these arrangements will be reviewed.

12. Children are entitled to support services that meet their assessed needs. These include advice and counselling, health, education, leisure, and cultural services, and practical and financial help when needed. Information from agency records will be made available to the child when they are of an age and level of understanding to comprehend it.

13. Where there are difficulties arising from an adoption or a proposed adoption, or where an adoption or proposed adoption breaks down, a child will receive support and information without delay.

14. Children placed for adoption and adopted children will be informed of their right to make representations and complaints and will be helped to do so if this is required.

B. Prospective Adopters

People who are interested in becoming adoptive parents will be welcomed without prejudice, responded to promptly and given clear information about recruitment, assessment and approval. They will be treated fairly, openly and with respect throughout the adoption process.

1. Information on becoming an adoptive parent will be provided, including what is expected of adopters. Applicants will be given the opportunity to hear about preparation and support services available to adopters, and to talk to others who have adopted children.

2. Clear information will be given about children locally and across the country who need families to help prospective adopters decide whether to proceed further.

3. Written eligibility criteria and details of the assessment and approval process will be provided.

   a) Applicants will be considered in terms of their capacity to look after children in a safe and responsible way that meets their developmental needs. Where agencies have specific eligibility criteria e.g. because the agency has particular religious beliefs, applicants will be told what these are and, if necessary, be referred to another agency. People will not be automatically excluded on the grounds of age, health or other factors, except in the case of certain criminal convictions.

   b) The assessment and approval process will be comprehensive, thorough and fair. An explanation will be given of the need for status checks and enquiries to be made about prospective adopters and members of their household.

4. There will be clear written timescales for each stage. Applicants can expect:

   a) Written information sent in response to their enquiry within 5 working days.

   b) Follow up interviews/invitation to an information meeting within 2 months

   c) Agencies will prioritise applications that are more likely to meet the needs of children waiting for adoption. Where agencies and applicants decide to proceed, a decision on the outcome will be made by the agency following the Adoption Panel within six months of the receipt of the formal application. Where the agency decides not to proceed applicants will be informed in writing and advised of the options open to them.

   d) If b) and c) follow each other without a gap, the whole process from enquiry to decision should not take more than 8 months. Panels will record reasons for delays.

5. Foster carers who make a formal application to adopt children in their care will be entitled to the same information and preparation as other adopters and be assessed within four months.

6. Applicants will be kept informed of progress throughout. They will receive a copy of the assessment report at least 28 days before an adoption panel and have the opportunity to comment on the report, and, if they wish, to attend the adoption panel and be heard.

7. Prospective adopters will be informed of their right to make representations and complaints.

C. Adoptive Parents

Children will be matched with approved adopters who can offer them a stable and permanent home and help and support will be provided to achieve a successful and lasting placement.

1. Approved adopters will be given clear written information about the matching, introduction and placement process, as well as any support to facilitate this that they may need. This will include the role of the Adoption Register for England and Wales.

2. Before a match is agreed, adopters will be given full written information to help them understand the needs and background of the child and an opportunity to discuss this and the implications for them and their family.

3. There will be access to a range of multi-agency support services before, during and after adoption. Support services will include practical help, professional advice, financial assistance v/here needed and information about local and national support groups and services.

4. Adoptive parents will be involved in discussions as to how they can best maintain any links, including contact, with birth relatives and significant others identified in the adoption plan.

5. Adoptive parents will be encouraged to keep safe any information provided by birth families via agencies and to provide this to the adopted child on request, or as they feel appropriate.

6. Adoptive parents whose adopted child has decided to explore their birth heritage will be supported to deal with the impact of this decision.

7. Where there are difficulties with the placement or the adoption breaks down the agencies involved will co-operate to provide support and information to the adoptive parents and the child without delay.

8. Agencies will ask adoptive parents whether they are prepared to agree to notify the agency if an adopted child dies during childhood or soon afterwards.

9. Adoptive parents will be informed of their right to make representations and complaints.

Reproduced with kind permission from Her Majesty's Stationery Office (HMSO).

Index